OWNABILITY

HOW INTELLECTUAL PROPERTY WORKS

**FOR ENTREPRENEURS
FREELANCERS ARTISTS
CREATIVES ENGINEERS
ILLUSTRATORS MAKERS
INVENTORS EXECUTIVES
PROGRAMMERS MUSICIANS
AUTHORS PHOTOGRAPHERS
AND** *you!*

BRENT C.J. BRITTON

DESIGN & ILLUSTRATION BY REUBEN & HUNTER

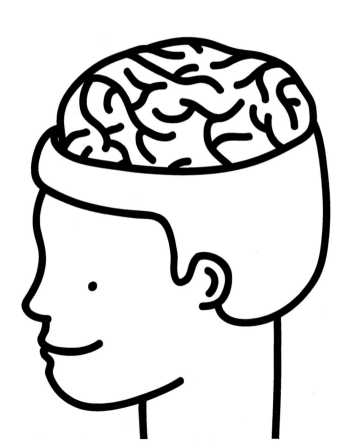

I wrote this book for my wonderful, amazing, creative clients to give them a bit of a roadmap to the legal landscape in which they work.

Most of my clients (and, frankly, most of the people I know) sit squarely in the creative class -- they create and invent and innovate for a living. Whether they are artists or engineers, executives or entrepreneurs, they are all driven to make the world a better place. Innovation is their primary focus; to succeed, they need to concentrate on innovating without getting too terribly bogged down in the convoluted details of business or law. Sure, they need to know a little bit -- just enough -- about how to conduct their business or their employment or what have you. But they shouldn't need to waste time becoming an expert in anything but creating and innovating!

I wrote this book to provide a "Goldilocks" description of Intellectual Property Law, one that's not too simple and not too complex. My hope is to impart just enough news you can use in a business context to get a handle on IP concepts without getting too heavily bogged down with needlessly prolix discussion of legal minutiae.

Ownability is the book I want to hand to my clients when they first come to me proclaiming to have created something amazing and wanting to explore how to protect it with IP. My hope is to have included just enough legal details to undergird productive legal discussions and business decisions about IP.

This book will not teach you everything IP law. But it will prepare you to speak more productively with your IP lawyer.

Read this book, then go change the world!

Ownability

When you create, design, or invent things, the rules of intellectual property (IP) determine who owns your creations and whether or not you can prevent other people from copying them. If you work in a creative or innovative field, you should know enough about IP to make intelligent decisions about your job or business. You should understand the ownability of your own ability.

This book provides a working understanding of the four primary forms of IP: patents, copyrights, trademarks, and trade secrets. You will learn what these forms of IP protect, how to obtain them, and how to avoid having them used against you by others.

Intellectual property is a complex subject; expertise in the field requires years of study and practice. By necessity, then, I have significantly simplified this material. This book will not prepare you to take the patent bar exam, but it will help you understand how IP can affect your life for better and for worse.

Table of Contents

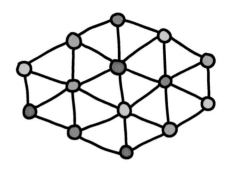

FIG. A

Copyrights   53

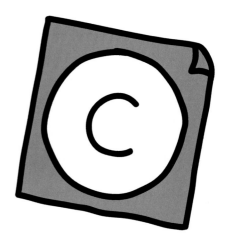

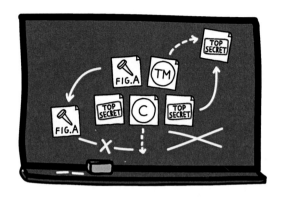

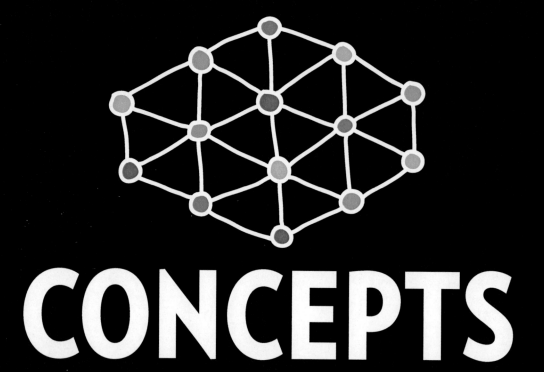

CONCEPTS

What You Will Learn...

Before diving deep into the details of trademarks, patents, copyrights, and trade secrets, let's walk through the general idea space. What is intellectual property and why is it important?

Intellectual property is everywhere. You can hardly exist in the modern world, let alone on the internet, without accessing or using someone's intellectual property.

The rules of intellectual property help you turn ideas into money, which, at its essence, is pretty much the goal of any creative or innovative business. Most productive companies can be thought of as little machines that take ideas in one end and pump money out of the other end by turning those ideas into tangible assets that can be owned, protected, and ultimately sold for profit -- a process enabled and governed almost entirely by intellectual property law.

Today's so-called knowledge economy veritably demands a working knowledge of IP. In developed economies, the owners of a company – its shareholders – generally expect the company's management to seize every lawful opportunity to increase the company's valuation and reduce the company's risks. Intellectual property law provides an array of options for achieving these goals. The wise entrepreneur should therefore obtain an understanding of IP basics and treat IP as an important component of efforts to maximize both company valuation and shareholder wealth.

Thankfully, of course, not all artistic endeavors have a business or money-making focus; plenty of IP is created every day that is never intended for sale or profit. But even these non-commercial creations are governed by the rules of intellectual property, so it's a good idea for creators across the spectrum to become familiar with how IP works.

What IP Can Do For You

Here are just a few things that effective use of IP can do for you or your company:

- IP can help forestall competition;
- IP can help reduce risks, including the risk of losing many types of lawsuits;
- IP can generate cash;
  and, perhaps most importantly,
- IP can help create new assets where none had existed before.

Let's briefly consider each of these in turn.

Forestall Competition

If you own comprehensive IP rights in your products, you can potentially prevent your competitors from copying, making, using, and selling equivalent products or otherwise trading on your success.

Reduce Risk

If you launch a product or service without first determining whether or not it might infringe any existing IP owned by your competitors, you are subjecting yourself to great risk of infringement liability.

Generate Cash

All IP rights can be carved up and licensed out to others, even competitors, for royalties and other payments.

Create New Assets

If you invent something, the invention is an asset. If you then get a patent on the invention, the patent becomes another asset, potentially a more valuable one. This accumulation of assets in your IP portfolio can contribute meaningfully to the overall valuation of your company.

Importance of IP

IP is the ROI on R&D – it's the reward you get for investing in innovation and design. Effective use of IP can create substantial value. Any enterprise that creates, innovates, designs, invents, or advances the state of the art in any technology should consider protecting its creations, innovations, designs, inventions, and advancements by obtaining all available IP rights. Aggressive, consistent attention to IP should be a core practice for businesses and solo artists alike. Creators of every size and flavor can use IP to fatten their valuation and thin their risk profile. Assets as prosaic as a brand name and a customer list can be protected by IP. Nearly every company and working artist owns such items and can use IP to protect them.

Of course, it may or may not turn out to be an intelligent or ethical decision for you to **assert** your IP rights against other people (by suing them) once those rights are obtained. But that should not stop you from **obtaining** all the IP rights to which you are entitled. You can always opt not to sue people. But you will never have a chance to decide whether or not to sue them if you neglect to obtain IP rights in the first place.

What Is IP?

What is intellectual property and why does it matter?

In a nutshell, intellectual property refers to the new things you and all innovators create, alongside the rights that protect those creations from being copied or used by competitors. We'll go over this in more detail shortly.

The U.S. Constitution enshrines the venerable western tradition of promoting intellectual property in its enumerated congressional powers. Article 1, Section 8 reads, in relevant part:

> Congress shall have the power to promote the progress of science and the useful arts by securing for limited times to authors and inventors the exclusive right to their respective writings and discoveries.

This Constitutional provision forms the basis for how we treat IP in the United States (a foundational proposition shared in more or less the same form throughout the modern world). It says that we should give people who take the trouble to create things a period of time during which they alone can profit from their creations. The Constitutional framers assumed that our country's government would increase the innovative output of its citizenry by granting IP rights to the people who create innovative or artful things. This Constitutional mandate assumes that the exclusive right to exploit new creations for limited times sufficiently encourages innovation among the people. It assumes that innovation means progress and that progress is something governments should promote.

For there can be no doubt that innovation drives progress in a capitalist democracy like the United States. With no new inventions, designs, or art we would stagnate. Without a constant stream of innovative new products and services, we would end up with nothing to trade with the rest of the world but the same old things we traded yesterday. And, with very few exceptions, if there is one thing the world will tire of, it is the same old thing.

On the flip side, any business that can manage to invent new things and convince the rest of us all to buy those things stands to obtain wealth and economic power;

any artist that develops and distributes successful works of art can touch the lives of billions of people.

Our country's founders had the foresight to recognize that a nation will grow in proportion to the energy and spirit of its creative class. Our intellectual property laws are not recent inventions of corporate America intended, as some would suggest, to hinder innovation and to maintain a *status quo* in which the little guy cannot hope to succeed against entrenched behemoths. On the contrary, our IP laws were envisioned at the dawn of our nation as a means for promoting progress, for oiling the wheels of capitalism, and for leveling the playing field among all innovators. Our IP laws apply equally to solo inventors and large companies alike.

Entrepreneurs and artists create things, at least in part, for economic reward. As one such reward, the intellectual property regime gives creators the exclusive right to enjoy the fruits of their labor, for a time. If you're intelligent or resourceful enough to create new things, we've agreed to thank you by letting you (or your employer) be the only person in the country who gets to make, use, sell, exploit, and enjoy the results and proceeds of those new things. Not everyone agrees that this philosophy is ideal or even that it works at all as described above. I discuss this at greater length at the end of the book.

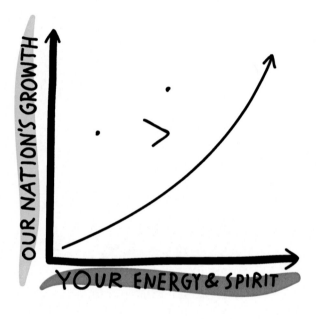

Important Definitions

I've been using the term Intellectual Property (and its acronym, IP) fairly casually up until now. IP is primarily a legal regime, however, and legal discussions require precision. Before we continue, therefore, let's clarify our definitions.

Intellectual Property Assets

Intellectual Property Assets are things you create. They include inventions, brands, works of authorship, and confidential information. [1]

Intellectual Property Rights

Intellectual Property Rights are powers created by governments and bestowed upon you to allow you to protect IP assets. Patents protect inventions, trademarks protect brands, copyrights protect works of authorship, and certain proprietary rights protect confidential information.

So IP rights protect IP assets. As a helpful analogy, consider that, under the laws governing the ownership of houses (that is to say *real* property as opposed to *intellectual* property), the **asset** would be your house, and the deed would represent your exclusive **right** of ownership in the house, which right includes the power to thwart trespassers. Likewise under intellectual property law, the **asset** is the invention or the brand, for example, and the **right** is the patent or trademark, respectively, representing your exclusive right to exploit the asset and to prevent other people from treading on it in various ways.

Intellectual Property Law

And finally, Intellectual Property Law is the set of rules established and enforced by governments that enable people and companies to own and assert IP rights to protect their IP assets.

Thus, IP **law** dictates that IP **rights** protect IP **assets**. What could be simpler? Owing to this overloading of the term "IP" inherent in the lexicon, references here and elsewhere to "IP" alone should be examined carefully to ascertain whether the writer is referencing IP assets, IP rights, IP law, or the general area of study.

This list and the list of corresponding rights immediately following are not exhaustive, but cover about 99% of the IP you are likely to deal in.

The Right of Exclusive Ownership

I've been saying that IP rights *protect* IP assets, but what does this really mean? In short, intellectual property rights give you rights of exclusive ownership, which means you alone become the sole owner of your creation. If someone else copies your creation, you can invoke your IP rights to make them stop. IP rights are therefore tools that can be asserted to help you prevent other people from copying your IP assets and competing against you in certain ways. IP rights work by giving you standing to bring lawsuits against people who might be abusing or misusing your IP. In fact, to be clear, that's how you enforce IP rights: by suing people who infringe them.

So, for example, if somebody infringes your patent, the patent doesn't automatically make the infringer stop. The patent gives you standing to bring a lawsuit against them for patent infringement. Likewise, if somebody infringes your copyright, misappropriates your trade secret, or infringes your trademark, those IP rights give you standing to bring a lawsuit against the wrongdoers. That is how such rights help you to prevent others from using and exploiting the intellectual property assets you have created, by giving you the right to sue them, to obtain awards such as money damages from them, and to obtain court injunctions that order the infringement to stop.

You enforce your IP rights only by suing infringers (or threatening to). You can get patents and copyrights all day long, but that won't do much to stop your competitors from copying things. To stop them, you have to assert your IP rights against them. In court. Often in the company of lawyers.

This important fact often comes as a bit of a surprise to first-time IP holders, who sometimes believe that merely **obtaining** IP rights can by itself prevent their competitors from copying their IP assets. "They can't copy me, I have a patent!" such folks often exclaim when they first sit down with counsel. The truth is they can copy you as long as they want until you assert your patent or other IP rights against them.

At the risk of overtaxing the real property metaphor, if IP assets are like your home and garden, IP rights protect your assets less like a fence and more like a watchdog. Unlike a fence, IP rights do not automatically keep people from trespassing on your property. To serve their purpose IP rights must, like a watchdog, be more or less weaponized and directed at intruders who've crossed the line into your space.

If you have mistakenly assumed that your IP rights are actively protecting you against copyists, take heed: **there is no godlike umpire out there roaming the planet seeking out infringers of your IP and automatically putting a stop to it**. Quite the contrary.

In order to stop someone from using or copying your IP, you've got to convince or force them to stop. And the way you usually do that is by suing them (or threatening to).

IP rights do not stop infringers from infringing; lawsuits do.

Intellectual property rights do not give you the right to succeed in business or to enjoy any particular level financial success. A patent is not a panacea; it is nothing more than a ticket into court. One does not succeed (or fail) in business merely by obtaining IP rights and then calmly sitting back and waiting for the royalty checks to start magically rolling in and all competition to magically cease. For a company to profit from its creations and win in the marketplace, it needs to do all the things successful companies do to manufacture, market, and sell products and services. IP can help with the success of those efforts by empowering you to clear an exclusive path to market, but IP rights alone almost never guarantee commercial success. IP rights are merely tools that can be used to sue people.

Value of Corporate Assets: Tangible vs. Intangible

The vast majority of corporate assets in the United States today are not hard assets, they are intellectual property assets. In 1970, some 80% of overall corporate assets were hard, tangible assets (such as desks and factories and trucks and other physical items) and only 20% were intangible (such as intellectual property). By 1997, this ratio had inverted, and it remains so to this day: roughly 75% of overall corporate assets today are intangible and only 25% are tangible. Most assets owned by companies are intellectual property assets. IP as an asset class represents most of the value in our economy.

Sometimes, IP can be more valuable than the underlying business it protects. For example, in 2003, a company called Gemstar, which owned TV Guide and a portfolio of intellectual property associated with the delivery of television-related information, was worth more than the four major television networks combined. In other words, the intellectual property holder in the television information delivery industry was worth more than the combined value of all of the major operators in that industry.
Which would you rather be?

VALUE OF
CORPORATE ASSETS

1970

80%   20%

TODAY

25%   75%

TYPES OF INTELLECTUAL PROPERTY

Let's consider the types of IP available to you, beginning with this basic overview. Then we'll go into more detail in each area.

Trademarks

If you create, own, or deal in brands, names, logos, or taglines – and pretty much every company has at least one of these – then you need to be cognizant of issues relating to **trademarks**. Trademarks protect brands. A brand is the name of a company or the name of a product or service. Brands are the words, phrases, logos, and other marks that identify the source of goods and services in the marketplace. Trademark rights are obtained by using the underlying brand in commerce. Registration is optional, but advised. A trademark lasts for as long as the underlying brand is used in commerce.

Patents

If you create, own, or deal in technological or scientific inventions, new business methods, software, certain designs, and certain other inventive creations, you need to be aware of the laws relating to **patents**. If you are inventing new things or advancing the state of the art in some technology, then you may be able to obtain patent protection for those things and advances. Patents protect inventions, processes, some designs, gene sequences, business methods, some plants, and software. Patents are obtained by inventing the invention and by applying for and being awarded a patent. Registration is mandatory. Patents in useful inventions last for 20 years, and 14 years for designs, from the date the application is filed, in the U.S.

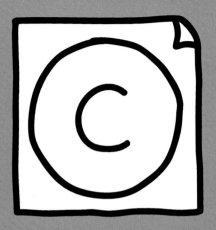

Copyrights

If you create, own, or deal in digital or analogue media, art, music, film, stories, written works, photographs, architectural works, choreography, sculpture, software, or other audiovisual works, you should know the rules regarding **copyrights**. Copyrights protect works of authorship – things that have an author. You obtain a copyright simply by just creating the work, by fixing it in a tangible form. Registration is optional, but advised. Copyright protection lasts for the life of the author plus 70 years, for works authored by a person. For works authored by companies, known as "works for hire," copyright protection lasts for 95 years from the date of first publication or 120 years from the date of creation if the work is never published.

Trade Secrets

If you create, own, or deal in confidential information, secrets, or know-how – in other words, if you use confidential information that has value because you know it and nobody else does – then you should pay attention to **trade secret** law. Trade secrets protect valuable secrets, such as ingredients, techniques, plans, customer lists, and the source code form of software. Trade secrets are obtained by keeping them secret, and they last for as long as you manage to keep them secret.

TRADEMARKS

What You Will Learn...

Trademarks are enormously valuable commercial assets. This discussion covers what trademarks are, how to obtain them, and how they can be infringed.

Trademarks protect brands, and are, therefore, critically important corporate assets. Your brand distinguishes your goods and services over those of your competitors and it thereby engenders the avoidance of consumer confusion. If a competitor were to use a brand that is confusingly similar to yours, this would presumably draw business away from you by confusing your customers into thinking they were purchasing your product when mistakenly purchasing your competitor's product. The confused consumer might thereby formulate an opinion as to the quality of your goods unjustifiably based on the (presumably lesser, but at any rate *different*) quality of your competitor's goods. The wisdom of protecting your brand with trademark rights therefore becomes quite clear.

Think of a well-known trademark, perhaps the word "Google" or the Nike swoosh or the McDonalds golden arches or the letters "IBM." Envisioning these trademarks in your mind's eye causes all sorts of images and feelings and emotions to cascade through your cranium, does it not? You know what these trademarks mean to you as a consumer; you know what you're going to get when you patronize the businesses these trademarks represent. You know what you think of other people when you see them using these brands, and you have a suspicion about what other folks think of you when they see you using these brands. In some cases, just by imagining the brand, you can almost feel, taste, and smell the goods represented.

In short, trademarks comprise a shorthand representation in your mind for the quality of the experience of being a consumer of the underlying goods or services. This makes trademarks extremely powerful consumer motivators.

Lest you think I overstate the case, consider the following fascinating scientific experiment that starkly demonstrates the surprisingly thorough influence trademarks can exert.

16

The Baylor Experiment

In 2004, Dr. Read Montague of Baylor College in Houston conducted an ingenious study wherein a group of people were asked to take a blind taste test between Coke and Pepsi. In the experiment, each of the participants took a sip of both Coke and Pepsi without knowing which drink was which. Each participant was then asked to name a preference. The result? When people did not know what they were drinking, roughly 50% said they preferred Coke and roughly 50% said they preferred Pepsi. The results were split right down the middle.

Then, Dr. Montague re-administered the experiment with the respective Coke and Pepsi trademarks exposed to the participants, so that they were confronted with the brands and thereby knew whether they were drinking Coke or Pepsi as they drank it. Under these circumstances, roughly 75% of the people said they preferred Coke, a full 25% more of the lot than under the blind test. Half of the Pepsi drinkers changed their answer when they knew what brand they were drinking.

What does this incredible result mean? In the second test, 25% of the people who took the test changed their answer out of loyalty to the Coke trademark. As proven by the first, blind test, the people who changed their answer from Pepsi to Coke, *clearly preferred the taste of Pepsi*. When they didn't know what they were drinking, they preferred the taste of Pepsi. But later when they knew they were drinking Coke, they *claimed to like Coke better*.

Did they lie? Did the people who changed their stated preference lie in order to ally themselves with the Coke brand? The only thing that changed between the two tests was the revelation of the trademarks. The chemical composition of the sodas did not change. The only way the participants could have changed their preference from Pepsi to Coke was due to the influence of the trademark – they lied out of brand loyalty.

That people would lie about their preferences out of sheer brand loyalty would be an illuminating example of the power of a brand, and a signifier of the importance of obtaining trademark rights to ensure brands are protected. The result gets even more interesting, however. When Dr. Montague's team administered these tests, the participants wore MRI scanners on their heads, which enabled the scientific team to examine their brain activity as the tests were being carried out. What they found is both fascinating and unsettling.

It turns out that many of the 25% of the test subjects who, when blind, preferred the taste of Pepsi, but *claimed* that they preferred Coke when they could see the trademark, might not have been lying after all. By studying the brain activity appearing in the MRI results, Montague's team determined that these subjects actually felt more pleasure drinking Coke when they knew it was Coke than they did when the trademark was hidden. When Coke drinkers knew they were drinking Coke, the pleasure centers in their brains fired more vigorously. Let me restate this amazing result: *some people physiologically enjoyed the experience of consuming the product more when they associated it with its trademark; when the trademark was not present, they enjoyed the product less, and actually preferred another product.* The participants got more physical pleasure out of drinking Coke when they knew it was Coke. Without the Coke trademark around to influence them, they liked Pepsi better.

One can scarcely imagine a more compelling demonstration of the power of trademarks. When you develop a brand, initiate it into commerce, and start getting customers to associate the brand with your products, this activity can potentially have a permanent physical effect on your customers' brains and bodies. In this way, you and your company can become physically bonded to your customers through your brand and the image the brand creates in their minds, both consciously and at realms inaccessible to conscious influence.

Given the power that the brand can wield, you would be wise to ensure that your brands are well protected by trademark rights and thus made more likely to contribute to the long term success of your products and services.

Samuel M. McClure, Jian Li, Damon Tomlin, Kim S. Cypert, Latané M. Montague, and P. Read Montague: "Neural Correlates of Behavioral Preference for Culturally Familiar Drinks." Published in Neuron, Volume 44, Number 2, October 14, 2004, pages 379–387

OBTAINING TRADEMARK PROTECTION

Trademark protection is relatively easy to obtain for a brand being used in commerce to identify the source of goods and services. In fact, merely using a brand in commerce generates a measure of protection and results in a so-called "common law" trademark or "state law" trademark. If you have been using a brand in commerce, but have not yet applied for federal trademark registration, you can still sue people who use a confusingly similar brand. But you can only sue them if they are using the confusingly similar brand in the geographic regions in which you are meaningfully using your brand. If you obtain a federal trademark registration, on the other hand, you can sue infringers anywhere in the U.S., whether or not you have business in the region. Thus, the preferable and more powerful alternative to a common law or state law trademark is, by far, a trademark that is registered with the U.S. Patent and Trademark Office.

Before we go into more detail on how to register trademarks, however, let's consider a couple of things that a trademark is not.

Trademark vs. Corporate Name

A trademark is different from a corporate name. Let's say you are starting a company called, "Purple Monkey Volcano, LLC." To begin, you will typically register the name of your company with the Secretary of State's office in the state of your choice. That act does not create a trademark. It is merely the Secretary of State's office authorizing you to operate a company that is named, "Purple Monkey Volcano, LLC." It doesn't mean you have the right to use that brand in commerce in your state or anywhere else without getting sued for trademark infringement by a prior user of a similar brand. It doesn't mean that "Purple Monkey Volcano" will turn out to be a particularly strong trademark, that your customers will like it, that it will contribute to the success of your business, or that you will be able to sue others who copy it. When the Secretary of State forms your company for you, that doesn't give you any trademark rights and it doesn't mean the secretary of state thinks you've chosen a protectable brand. It simply means that you have secured local ministerial permission to refer to your company as, in this example, "Purple Monkey Volcano, LLC." This has almost nothing to do with trademark rights.

In this regard, the Secretary of State is akin to a sign painter. Sign painters don't create trademarks; they simply paint words on boards. You can go visit the

local sign painter and request that he or she paint you a sign with the name, "Purple Monkey Volcano, LLC" on it. Great, now you'll own a sign. It will, perhaps, be a very lovely sign. But it won't mean that you will enjoy exclusive rights to the words painted on the sign or that you won't get sued for trademark infringement when you hang the sign outside your shop. And it doesn't mean you'll be able to sue anyone else if they use those words to brand their goods or services.

It simply means that you've bought and paid for a board with some words painted on it.

Reserving a corporate name with your Secretary of State's office confers no more trademark rights on your brand than having a sign painted.

Trademark vs. Domain Name

The same thing is true for an internet domain name. Obtaining a domain name has very little to do with trademark rights. It merely secures for you the name of a virtual address on which to build an online presence. When you register a domain name, the internet registrar has done little more than paint you a sign on the internet. Becoming the registrant of PurpleMonkeyVolcano.com doesn't mean you thereby enjoy any right to use the words in the domain name commercially without getting sued, and it doesn't mean that you can sue other people if they use those words.

To be clear: naming a company and registering a domain name neither establish trademark rights nor insulate you from attack by others. To do that, you need to do more than register a domain name or form a corporation; you need to use your brand name in commerce and accrue or establish trademark rights.

Clear Trademarks Rights Before Finalizing Company Names & Domain Names

Trademark rights must be considered *alongside* company name and domain name selection. Securing a suitable name for your company is hugely important, and the naming process is a critical step to corporate formation and internet presence. In an ideal world, these painted signs – the name of your company and the name of your internet address – would be more or less identical, as this would be likely to help customers find you more easily. But none of these things is any use whatsoever, and can ultimately prove to be counterproductive, unless trademark dynamics are integrated into the process.

Failing to consider trademark rights early can cause a needless waste of time and money. Suppose you go to the Secretary of State and form Purple Monkey Volcano LLC and then go out to a domain name registrar and purchase the PurpleMonkeyVolcanoLLC.com domain name. Naturally, you begin building your website using this name, ordering business cards and stationary with this name on them, and generally investing in similar assets and activities based on the assumption that you have firmly and finally selected your brand name. At some point you ask your lawyer to register the Purple Monkey Volcano brand as a trademark. The lawyer performs a trademark search and discovers that, oops, someone else already owns a registered trademark similar to Purple Monkey Volcano for use with similar goods and services! Your lawyer advises that your use of the mark would carry a high risk of infringing the senior user's trademark. You will have several options for responding to this news, but a very highly probable outcome of this unfortunate scenario will be that you will have to change your company's name. All of the work you've done and money you've spent on Purple Monkey Volcano domain names and marketing collateral will have been almost completely wasted.

Your trademark is the mark of your trade. It guards your brand, which is probably your most important outwardly facing asset. Everything your company does – every interaction your company has with its customers – is represented in those customers' heads by your brand. Don't make the mistake of thinking you enjoy trademark rights in your brand without taking the steps necessary to establish those rights, as discussed below.

Trademark Searches

A trademark search is an essential step in choosing a brand name. When performed by competent legal counsel, a trademark search results in a legal opinion as to whether using the proposed brand will infringe anyone else's existing mark, and also whether you will be likely to obtain a trademark registration for the brand yourself. Note that registration and infringement are two separate questions. It is entirely possible that the United States Patent and Trademark Office (USPTO) will allow registration for a mark that nonetheless ends up infringing an existing trademark, for example, or that a mark with very low infringement risk nonetheless remains unlikely to qualify for registration.

Knock-Out Searching

Because a professional trademark search and accompanying legal opinion can cost $2000 or more, however, you may wish to consider conducting your own so-called "knock-out" search prior to engaging a lawyer. Conduct a knock-out search by using the trademark search features available at http://www.uspto.gov, alongside your internet search engine of choice, to identify existing uses of the mark in commerce by other companies. The point of a knock-out search is to establish whether there appear to be any existing companies using your proposed brand to identify themselves as the source of goods and services similar to yours. If such users exist, it may be best to knock this proposed brand out of the running and to start over with another brand without bothering to engage legal counsel. If no similar users are found in a knock-out search, on the other hand, it may be worth asking counsel to proceed with a formal trademark search.

Once a trademark search and opinion letter have been obtained and you are satisfied with the levels of risk associated with using the mark in commerce and attempting to register it, you can proceed to file a trademark application.

Qualifying for Trademark Protection

To be considered worthy of trademark protection, a company's brand name must be considered "fanciful." Fanciful means that the name should be a made-up word (e.g. "Google") or that it should be an existing word arbitrarily applied to dissimilar goods or services (e.g. "Apple" computers). To qualify for the strongest trademark protection, a brand name should not be suggestive or descriptive of the company's underlying goods and services. Competitors will also need to use words that are descriptive of their goods and services to be able to compete fairly in the ordinary course of business – literally to describe their products. So a single company may not own those descriptive words to the exclusion of its competitors.

For example, Apple Computer can probably trademark the word *apple* because, among other things, the word *apple* bears no descriptive relationship to computers. It is arbitrary in the context of computers. Likewise, Apple Records can also probably trademark the word *apple* with respect to records for the same reasons.

A company that operates an apple orchard may **not** trademark the word *apple*, however, because the word *apple* is generically descriptive of the underlying apple orchard-related products and services. All of the orchard's competitors in the apple industry will necessarily have to use the word *apple* to describe their business. It would be unfair to permit a single competitor to own the words that generically describe the underlying business.

The practical result of the rules requiring that trademarks be fanciful as opposed to descriptive is that if you want to adopt a strong trademark – one that more distinctively identifies you and can be used to thwart confusingly similar uses – you should select a brand that has little or no rhetorical relation to the words used to describe your underlying goods and services. To the contrary, trademarks that are very descriptive of the underlying goods and services will be considered weak marks that confer little or no protection to the brand.

LAPTOPS,INC

APPLE COMPUT

Different Kinds of Trademarks

When filing a trademark application, you can elect to register the brand as a **standard character mark** or as a **design mark**. Brands can be composed of words (such as "Nike"), logos (such as the Nike swoosh), and slogans (such as "Just Do It") because all of these things can be used to identify Nike, Inc. as the source of its athletic wear and other goods in the marketplace. Brands can also be composed of combinations of words and designs – words or other elements that are used in particular fonts or that have a particular stylized appearance (such as the words "Coca-Cola" in the fancy red and white script appearing on most Coke bottles and cans). Standard character trademark registration is available only for those brands consisting entirely of words and letters, while design mark protection is available for all brands, regardless of their composition.

A standard character mark confers greater strength than a design mark, as it will protect the underlying brand from being infringed by any use of the letters and other alphanumeric characters composing the brand, regardless of how their appearance is stylized in the infringing use. A design mark, on the other hand, only protects against depictions of the brand that are visually similar to the trademarked design. That is, the owner of a design mark can only sue those who are using a similar font, style, or visual appearance of the words or other elements in the trademarked design. Thus, **owning a standard character trademark in a brand provides broader protection than owning a design mark in the same brand**. Filing for design mark protection may be wise, however, in cases where registration of the brand as a character mark is unavailable or weak.

STANDARD CHARACTER MARK

DESIGN MARK!

Colors & Sounds as Trademarks

You can own a color as a trademark if the color is strongly enough associated with your business. For example, a certain shade of the color pink is owned by Owens Corning for use as the color of home fiberglass insulation, known in the trade as the "pink stuff." If you plan to go into the home insulation business, you may not sell insulation colored pink, because customers would likely be confused into believing that your pink product was the trademarked "pink stuff" sold by Owens Corning. Likewise, a certain shade of the color brown is owned by United Parcel Service for the color of the trucks that deliver parcel packages and the uniforms of the people who drive them. Competitors in the package delivery business may not color their trucks or uniforms that color brown. When a delivery truck pulls up and customers see its brown color, they know immediately that the UPS truck has arrived. If a UPS competitor pulled up in a truck that color, the customers would incorrectly assume that they were seeing a UPS truck and entrusting their packages to UPS for delivery.

Interestingly, some sounds can be owned as trademarks if they are distinctive enough to categorically identify the source of goods or services. The so-called NBC chimes (the notes G-E-C played in succession), for example, and the THX theatrical sound system promo's "deep note" sound have been registered in the U.S. as trademarks.

Product Design Features as Trademarks = Trade Dress

A form of trademark protection known as "trade dress" can protect the design features of products and packaging. Trade dress protection does not apply to standard character words, logos, or taglines. Instead, trade dress attaches to distinctive shapes or design features of a product or its packaging. Examples include the classic ribbed "hourglass" Coke bottle, the elaborately festooned interior décor of a particular Mexican restaurant, and the distinctive shape of a Ferrari.

Consider trade dress protection if the design or packaging elements of your products possess such distinctiveness that they identify you as the source of your goods and services in the marketplace.[2]

Classes of Goods & Services; Specimens

The astute reader might be asking how Apple Computer and Apple Records can co-exist, each using the Apple brand. The answer lies in the fact that trademarks exist within distinct **classes** of goods and services.

Under the common law, if you use the Purple Monkey Volcano brand to sell, say, tacos, and another company uses the same brand to sell, say, dental tools, both of you can probably obtain trademark rights in the brand, each within your distinct class of goods and services. The reason? It is taken as unlikely that a consumer of Purple Monkey Volcano dental tools would be confused into thinking that Purple Monkey Volcano tacos originate from the same source. It is probably safe to assume that most manufacturers of dental tools do not produce tacos, and vice versa.

Designs are conceivably protectable with trade dress, copyright, and design patent rights. Consult with your IP counsel to determine the best method of protecting your designs. [2]

Interestingly, Apple Records and Apple Computer co-existed relatively peacefully until the time at which Apple Computer entered the music business in 2004 with the launch of iTunes. A lawsuit ensued, and the companies settled out of court.[3]

When applying to register a mark, you must specify at least one class of goods and services and also write a detailed description of the goods and services with which the mark is used. The class and the detailed description of goods and services will be used to demarcate the metes and bounds of your trademark rights – tacos or dental tools, as the case may be – within a reasonable zone of expansion.

Together with your trademark application, you will be required at some point to submit a **specimen** of the mark in use as a label on the products, or as an advertisement to promote the services, that you specified in the statement of goods and services. If a specimen is not yet available, you may wish to file an **Intent-To-Use application**, which can help to establish trademark rights for a mark that is not yet in use.

In any trademark application, but especially in the context of an Intent-To-Use application, be exceedingly careful in your selection of trademark class and your description of goods and services to ensure that they exactly match the specimen you eventually submit.

Many trademark applicants have run into trouble by misidentifying these items owning either to undue haste or reliance on assumptions about future products that later prove to be inaccurate. Choosing trademark classes and drafting descriptions of goods and services can be delicate. Think very carefully before deciding. Are you selling a product (say, a downloadable software product), or a service (say, the right to **access and use** a web-based software system)? If you establish trademark rights in the PurpleMonkeyVolcano brand for dental tools, would it upset you to find that someone else has come along selling PurpleMonkeyVolcano brand tacos? You are strongly urged to consult with competent trademark counsel to identify these questions and answer them to your liking.

[3] Apple Corps Limited v. Apple Computer, Inc., [2006] England and Whales High Court 996 (Chancery Division)

TRADEMARK APPLICATION PROCESS

Once filed, a U.S. trademark application gets reviewed by a trademark examiner at the Patent and Trademark Office in Washington D.C., a process that can take several months. Be patient. Eventually, the examiner will take one of two steps: 1. issue an office action; or 2. allow the registration.

By the way, do not be alarmed if your lawyer refers to this process as trademark "prosecution." In this context, prosecution is just a fancy word for processing; it has nothing to do with criminal prosecution. It does, however, belie the fact that the filing of a trademark application establishes what can best be thought of as an adversarial relationship between the applicant, who seeks to obtain the broadest possible trademark protection for the brand, and the USPTO examiner, who seeks to permit only the most worthy brands to obtain only as little trademark protection as is legally justified.

Office Actions

In response to the vast majority of all trademark applications filed, the USPTO examiner issues an office action, which is a recitation of the reasons why the examiner refuses to allow the registration. The applicant has six months to respond to an office action either by taking the steps, if any, suggested by the examiner to overcome the objections, or by arguing on the points raised by the examiner to advocate for a different result or interpretation. When the office action response is filed, the process iterates and the examiner can either allow the mark or issue another – final – office action, from which an appeal to a higher authority is possible, but often costly.

Trademark Registration Allowance

Once the trademark examiner decides to allow registration of a trademark, the mark is published for opposition for a 30-day period in which anyone in the public who feels they would be  harmed by registration of the mark may oppose the registration. While it is rare for anyone to oppose a well-researched trademark application, it does occur. When an opposition is filed, the applicant must commit resources to responding to the opposition or potentially lose the trademark. The applicant can thus be faced with an adversarial dispute on par with a trademark infringement litigation. If you receive notice that an opposition has been filed against your trademark application, seek the advice of competent intellectual property counsel immediately.

Issuance

If an intent-to-use application is prosecuted to the point where the trademark registration has been allowed and is about to issue, the applicant may then file a declaration of use together with a specimen of the mark in use, or may file for a 6-month extension of time to do so. If the mark remains out of use, the applicant may file up to five additional 6-month extensions. By the expiration of the final extension, the applicant must file a declaration of use and a specimen of the mark in use, or the application will be abandoned. Yes, this means you can file an intent-To-Use trademark application today, see it through to allowance, and then wait another three years before filing a specimen of the mark in use in commerce.

Once a trademark application survives any office actions and any opposition process, and a valid specimen and declaration of use have been filed, the trademark is registered and a certificate of registration is issued to the applicant. A trademark registration in the U.S. lasts for 10 years, and is renewable for subsequent 10-year periods for as long as the mark is used in commerce. The registrant must file a declaration of continued use between the 5th and 6th years after registration. This filing keeps the registration alive and enhances the strength of the trademark.

Trademark Infringement

Under what circumstances can a trademark holder bring suit against an infringer? The trademark holder can bring a lawsuit against anyone who uses a similar mark in a way that is likely to confuse consumers as to the source of its goods and services. Basically, if the brands are similar and the goods or services are similar, then the infringing user of the brand will probably be required to yield to the trademark holder.

Originality

Interestingly, a trademark infringer needn't have any knowledge that its use of a brand infringes a trademark in order to be found liable for trademark infringement. In legal parlance, the defendant needn't have acted knowingly or with any intent to infringe. *An infringer need not intentionally be infringing a trademark to lose a trademark infringement lawsuit.* They can be infringing it by mistake and yet still qualify as a valid defendant. You can sue "innocent" trademark infringers. The originality of the genesis of the infringer's brand is no defense.

You can also be sued yourself, even if you are an "innocent" trademark infringer having no clue that you've infringed anything. Indeed, some people accused of trademark infringement often react to the accusation by protesting that they couldn't possibly be infringing anything because they haven't *copied* anything. They protest that they themselves thought up their brand name all on their own and had no knowledge of the accuser's trademark, and so they ask how they can possibly infringe what they did not copy. In so doing, they make the mistake of assuming that liability for trademark infringement requires them to have acted with intent – to have purposefully attempted to duplicate someone else's trademark. They assume that the originality of the genesis of their own brand matters. It doesn't. As noted, intent to infringe is not required. *If you are using a brand name that is confusingly similar to the brand name of another company who began using it first on similar goods or services, that company can sue you for trademark infringement and potentially win, even if you've never before heard of them or their trademark and even if you created your brand without copying theirs.* This underscores the importance of performing a comprehensive trademark search prior to committing valuable resources to a new brand name. It is your obligation to know what's out there in your competitive brand space and to actively steer clear of existing marks.

MATTERS TO CONSIDER AFTER REGISTRATION

Generally, trademarks remain in force for as long as they are used in commerce. Here are a few items to pay attention to after you get your trademark to ensure it remains as strong as possible.

Active Policing

Trademark holders are encouraged to police others' uses of similar trademarks and pursue those who are likely to create a likelihood of confusion in the marketplace. Owning a trademark is similar to owning real property in this regard. If a land owner allows people to walk across her land long enough, she may eventually lose the right to stop them from walking across it. In the same way, if you as a trademark holder sit idly by while others use confusingly similar brands or otherwise infringe your trademark, you may potentially lose the right to enforce your trademark against anyone.

For example, suppose you own the Purple Monkey Volcano trademark and you know of three companies that are using confusingly similar – potentially infringing – brands in the marketplace. But, for whatever reasons, you choose not to attack them. Perhaps they don't seem to be causing too much competitive turmoil, or they aren't earning enough money from the infringement to make them a lucrative litigation target, or what have you. You let them go. Then, months or years later, you learn of a fourth infringer, and, again perhaps because you suspect there's more gold in them thar' hills, you elect to file suit against this one.

What will the defendant – this fourth known infringer of your trademark, but the first you've sued – what will this company likely argue in its defense? It will probably attempt to convince the judge or jury that your lawsuit isn't particularly fair. It will argue that it believed its actions to be lawful since at least three other companies were infringing your brand without consequence. The defendant may claim that it is only being singled out because it has deep pockets and not because you are truly concerned about protecting your trademark. Thus, counsel may advise you not to cherry pick but instead to pursue lawful remedies against all infringers as they come to light.

Genericide

A thorough approach to trademark strategy includes something known as "genericide". Genericide is the destruction of trademark rights by virtue of, oddly, the overwhelming popularity of the underlying brand! A brand can sometimes become so popular that it morphs into a generic substitute name for the entire class of goods and services to which it belongs. Examples of this include yo-yo, allen wrench, escalator, touchtone, linoleum, and aspirin. These words were once trademarked brand names that were owned exclusively, each by a single company; you could once have purchased Yo-Yo brand toys, Escalator brand moving stars and Aspirin brand painkiller. Over time, because of the immense popularity of these brands, they became generic terms used to describe the entire class of goods to which they belong, so that today you can purchase yo-yos, escalators, and aspirin made by numerous competitors.

When asked what trademarks that are in use today might be in danger of becoming victims of genericide, most people mention Coke, Band-Aid, Xerox, Kleenex, and Q-tips. These are, as you might expect, very well-known brands, which have added considerable value

- BAND-AID
- COKE
- KLEENEX
- FRISBEE
- YO-YO

to their respective owners' bottom lines. Genericide, while unfortunate, nonetheless indicates great success in the marketplace. It may therefore seem as though a company could endure many worse problems than trademark genericide. Indeed, we should all be so lucky in business that our trademarks become so extraordinarily popular that the general public begins to conceive of them as substitutes for the whole market sector they represent.

Unfortunately, however, trademark genericide remains a very real and costly threat to successful companies. One can scarcely imagine a more tragic injury to The Coca-Cola Company, for example, than to lose exclusive ownership rights in its Coke brand and consequently to lose the ability to prevent its competitors from labeling their products "Cokes." To prevent this, Coca-Cola has waged a costly and sustained effort to ensure that the word Coke is not used as a generic substitute for all sodas. If too many people receive a Pepsi after ordering a Coke, the Coke brand risks becoming genericized as a generic substitute for all colas. It is for this reason that waiters ask, "Is Pepsi OK?" when you order a Coke in a restaurant that serves Pepsi products; the Coca-Cola Company makes them say it.

Trademark Symbols

The symbol for a registered trademark is ®, which is typically superscripted to the right of the mark. You should use ® as soon as your trademark is registered. You should not use ® until you actually own a registered trademark, however. You own a registered trademark when you receive a certificate from the USPTO that says you do, and not a moment sooner. It is fraudulent to use ® until you have received a certificate of registration from the USPTO.

The "TM" symbol can be used with common law trademarks that are not yet registered, as can the "SM" symbol. TM stands for trademark, and SM stands for service mark; **they can be used with no registration as soon as you enter a product or service into commerce**. They can also be used interchangeably. Generally, if you see yourself as being in a product business, use TM, and if you see yourself as being in a service business, use SM.

Most companies use TM, since most customers know what TM means, whereas SM is less familiar. It is good practice to use TM or SM on every use of your brand unless and until it is registered, because this puts the world on notice that you believe your brand qualifies as a trademark and that you intend to enforce it.

Final Thoughts on Trademarks

Ultimately, the amount of resources and effort you direct to the establishment and maintenance of trademark rights should be directly proportional to the value of your brand name. If you consider your brand to be a meaningful contributor to your ability to attract customers and keep them happy, it would be foolhardy not to protect your brand as thoroughly as possible by availing yourself of the advantages afforded by trademark law.

PATENTS

What You Will Learn...

The U.S. Patent and Trademark Office issues a million new patents every few years. Surely, then, if you're inventing new products, patents are worth paying attention to. This chapter discusses what patents are, how they are obtained, and how they can be infringed.

Patents protect inventions. In the intellectual property context, inventions are devices, compositions of matter, or processes that are novel and non-obvious. When you invent something, the only way to prevent other people from making, using, or selling copies of your invention is to patent it.[4]

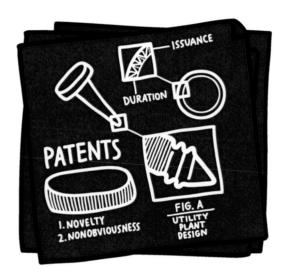

Technically, you can also attempt to prevent copying by keeping your invention secret, but this strategy is of limited use if you also hope to sell your invention to the public. [4]

OBTAINING A PATENT
REGISTRATION REQUIRED

Federal registration with the USPTO is required to obtain a patent. Mere creation or use of an invention is insufficient to confer exclusive rights in it to the inventor. Unlike with trademarks, no common-law or unregistered patent rights are available. Put another way, *registering a patent is the only way to obtain exclusive ownership of inventions and methods.* The inventor may, of course, own the physical embodiment of the invention – the parts and materials used to build it – and if someone were to take those physical things away, the inventor could attempt to bring a civil action or press criminal charges against the thief. But merely owning the physical materials gives the inventor no right to prevent another person or company from making, using, or selling copies of the invention. That you have built a new invention does not mean that you can necessarily stop anyone else from building something similar.

That requires a patent.

Patent Searches

Prior to filing a patent application, consider asking legal counsel to conduct a patentability search to help determine whether your invention is patentable. A patentability search involves a fairly thorough review of the so-called "patent prior art," which is comprised of the published U.S. patents and applications in the same field as your invention. Filing a patent application without first conducting a patentability search is a bit like traveling to a far-off city's only hotel without first calling to reserve a room. It's a long, expensive trip to take without knowing whether accommodations will be available when you finally arrive. In part because of the rather substantial investment of time and money involved in drafting and filing a patent application, a patent search is generally seen as an essential step in the patenting process.

A competent patent search should result in a legal opinion as to whether patent registration is likely to be obtained for the invention.[5] This process can result in a better understanding of the competitive landscape into which the invention is going to be injected. This, in turn, can help you refine the invention to make it more likely to be patentable, and possibly more competitive, in light of the prior art.

A professional patent search and accompanying legal opinion can cost $3000 or more, and can take 4 to 6 weeks to complete. The search can be extended beyond the patent prior art to cover relevant technical literature and even foreign patents and resources, but this adds considerably to the expense of time and money required. Consult with counsel to ascertain whether an expanded search is appropriate for you. In any case, once a competent patentability search has been performed and you have reviewed the opinion letter and are satisfied with the levels of risk associated with attempting to obtain a patent, you can proceed to file a patent application.

[5] Note that this is a separate question from whether making, using, or selling the invention is likely to infringe any existing patents, which is usually the subject of a separate undertaking and rarely combined with the patentability search. It is entirely possible that the USPTO could allow a patent for an invention that nonetheless ends up infringing an existing patent. A non-infringement opinion, also called a freedom-to-operate opinion, can cost ten times more than a patentability opinion.

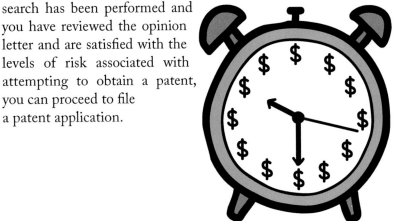

Requirements for Patentability

To be patentable, your invention must meet a few requirements.

Novelty

One requirement for patentability is novelty; your invention must be novel to warrant patent protection. The novelty requirement means that you must be the first person to have invented your invention and to have then filed a patent application on it. If the patent examiner at the USPTO finds a single reference in the prior art (such as an earlier patent or an article in a technical periodical) that recites all of the elements of your invention as claimed in your patent application, then your invention is not patentable for lack of novelty.

Nonobviousness

Another requirement for patentability is that your invention must be nonobvious. Where the novelty test just described lends itself to a measure of objectivity – either a single source disclosing all of the features of your invention can be found or it can't – the test for nonobviousness is a bit more subjective.

Technically, the statutory test for nonobviousness goes like this: A patent may not be obtained if the differences between the invention sought to be patented and the prior art are such that the invention as a whole would have been obvious at the time the invention was made to a person having ordinary skill in the field of the invention.

The circular nature of the statutory definition – an invention is nonobvious if it is not obvious – leaves the finer points of defining nonobviousness up to the courts. At present, U.S. courts hold that your invention may be obvious and not patentable if, in vastly oversimplified terms, an experienced person in your field, after taking a long hard look at the state of the art, would have predicted that your invention was coming along soon. In practice, this means that **patents should only be awarded to inventions that advance the state of the art in an unexpected, meaningful, or more than insignificant way**. To be nonobvious, your invention must be nontrivial. It helps if the invention satisfies a long unmet need of some kind, as demonstrated, perhaps, by market success.

To illustrate the difference between novelty and nonobviousness, suppose you learn of a new product called nanowire, which is a lightweight but very strong wire made of carbon nanofibers, so you go buy a spool of it, install it on your fishing pole, and use it as fishing line. Your invention is the nanowire fishing pole. Your invention may indeed be novel -- you may happen to be the first person in the world to buy a spool of nanowire and use it as fishing line. But your invention is probably obvious: any skilled angler would have seen the utility of using the new nanowire on a fishing pole. By doing so, you haven't really advanced the state of the art or transformed the off-the-shelf products into a new invention.

The obviousness analysis is often one of the most hotly contested issues in any patent prosecution. In the balance, it is reasonable to expect your patent attorney to expend considerable resources focusing on arguments against the examiner's actual or anticipated findings of obviousness.

Timing of Patent Filings

If you are planning to seek patent protection for an invention, remember that the clock is ticking. If you wait too long, you may be unable to get a patent. In the U.S., a patent application must be filed within one year after the first public use, disclosure, sale, or advertising of the invention. If you neglect to file a patent application within this one-year period, you thereby render your invention unpatentable.

Many foreign countries provide no such one-year grace period. In those countries – called absolute novelty jurisdictions – your invention loses patentability if you publicly disclose or sell your invention anywhere *at any time before filing* a patent application in any jurisdiction. If you are planning to seek patent protection in absolute novelty countries, be aware that any public disclosure or use of the invention before filing a patent application somewhere can terminate the novelty of the invention and thereby prevent patentability in those countries. To preserve patentability in foreign countries, therefore, it may be advisable to file a **provisional patent** in the U.S. as soon as possible to avoid inadvertent public disclosure or use of the invention prior to filing the (more time-consuming) nonprovisional patent application. See the discussion of provisional patents on page 45.

In the U.S. at present, the first inventor to file a patent application on an invention is the proper recipient of any patent that may be awarded on the invention, not necessarily the first to have invented it. If you have invented your invention but neglected to file a patent application, and then a competitor later invents the same invention and does file a patent application, you may lose your ability to obtain a patent on your invention. Filing quickly therefore becomes of primary importance.

The timing issues arising in the global patent context are complex and multidimensional. Failure to meet deadlines and abide by the various applicable rules can result in permanent loss of patent rights. Inventors are advised to consult with competent patent counsel to ensure maximum protection.

Different Kinds of Patents

Patents come in several different flavors, depending on their subject matter: *utility, plant, and design*. Patents can also be *provisional* or *nonprovisional*.

Utility, Plant, & Design Patents

Utility patents protect machines, methods, manufactured articles, and compositions of matter. Utility patents comprise the vast majority of all patent applications filed in the U.S. and the world.

Plant patents protect new breeds of certain kinds of plants and are most useful to those in the horticultural sciences.

Design patents protect the designs of manufactured articles, the surface ornamentation and aesthetic configuration of products.

Hmm... wait a minute, that part about aesthetic configuration sounds a lot like the earlier discussion of trade dress, doesn't it? Yes, as a matter of fact it does. The design of a product can be susceptible to both trade dress protection and design patent protection. Competent counsel can help you choose.

Provisional Patents

In the U.S., inventors can file a document known as a *provisional patent*, sometimes referred to as a provisional patent *application*. In truth, both names are misleading because a provisional patent is neither a patent nor an application for a patent. Strictly speaking, a provisional patent is merely a document that is filed with the USPTO in which the inventor describes an invention. That's it. This document is never examined or reviewed by the USPTO; it is merely placed on file for a year in anticipation of a follow-on nonprovisional patent application that is based on it. If, during the year after a provisional patent is filed, the inventor files a nonprovisional patent application on the invention disclosed in the earlier provisional patent that enables the same invention, the nonprovisional patent application will obtain the original filing date – called the priority date – of the provisional patent.

Nonprovisional patent applications generally cost around US $10,000 for patent counsel to prepare and file. Provisional patents, however, can be much less expensive. If prepared by counsel, a thorough provisional patent can run from US $3000 to US $4000. But because provisional patents are never examined, they can be much less rigorously prepared than nonprovisional applications; as the inventor, you are often in a great position to draft your own

provisional application asking counsel only to review before filing. This can reduce your fees to perhaps $500 or less.

Because a provisional patent can be prepared quickly and inexpensively, filing a provisional patent is useful when a company wishes to begin to obtain a measure of patent protection without committing to the expense of time and money required to prepare and file a nonprovisional patent application. After a provisional patent is filed, for example, **the inventor can use the phrase "patent pending"** when publicly referring to the invention disclosed in the provisional patent. This notice that a patent application is in the works can sometimes forestall others from copying the invention. Furthermore, a U.S. provisional patent qualifies as the kind of patent filing necessary to preserve the absolute novelty of the invention in certain non-U.S. jurisdictions, as discussed above.

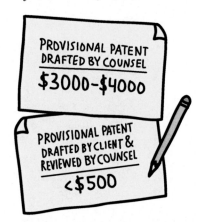

PROVISIONAL PATENT DRAFTED BY COUNSEL
$3000–$4000

PROVISIONAL PATENT DRAFTED BY CLIENT & REVIEWED BY COUNSEL
<$500

As a general rule, anyone doing a lot of inventing should be filing a lot of provisional patents. You can even include more than one invention in the same provisional while paying a single filing fee at the USPTO.

PATENT APPLICATION PROCESS

Once filed, a U.S. non provisional patent application gets reviewed by a patent examiner at the USPTO, a process that can take several years. Be patient. Depending on the subject matter of the patent application, a response may not come for 30 months or more. Eventually, the examiner will take one of two steps: 1. issue an office action; or 2. allow the patent to issue.

Again, as with trademarks, the process of arguing with the USPTO over whether or not the patent should issue is called patent "prosecution." Likewise, the patent prosecution process can be thought of as an adversarial relationship between the applicant, who seeks to obtain the broadest possible patent protection for the invention, and the USPTO examiner, who seeks to permit only the most worthy inventions to obtain the thinnest justifiable patent protection.

PATENT EXAMINER

Office Actions

In response to the vast majority of all patent applications filed, the examiner issues an office action, which is a recitation of the reasons why the examiner refuses to allow the patent. The applicant has six months to respond to an office action either by taking the steps, if any, suggested by the examiner to overcome the objections, or by arguing on the points raised by the examiner to advocate for a different result or interpretation. When the office action response is filed, the process iterates and the examiner can either allow the patent or issue another – final – office action, from which an appeal to a higher authority is possible, but often costly.

Patent Publication

Nonprovisional patent applications are kept confidential by the USPTO until 18 months after filing, whereupon they are published for all to read and review. This fact should figure prominently in the formulation of your IP strategy; while secrecy is available in certain circumstances, most patent applications become a matter of public record 18 months after they are filed, which is typically long before they ever issue as registered patents. Once published, the contents of a patent will never again be protectable as trade secrets.

Issuance & Duration

Once a patent application survives the examination process, the patent is granted and a certificate of registration is issued to the applicant. Utility and plant patents last for 20 years from the date the application was filed; design patents, for 14 years. Patents are not renewable. When they expire, the underlying invention becomes part of the public domain for all to make, use, and sell.

Patent Infringement

Under what circumstances can a patent-holder bring suit against an infringer? The patent holder may bring a patent infringement action against anyone who makes, uses, or sells the patented invention or its close equivalents.

Originality

As with trademarks, a patent infringer needn't have any knowledge that its use of an invention infringes a patent in order to be found liable for patent infringement. ***An infringer need not intentionally be infringing a patent to lose a patent infringement lawsuit.*** They can be infringing it by mistake and yet still qualify as a valid defendant. The infringer does not have to have formulated any intent to infringe. You can sue "innocent" patent infringers. The originality of the genesis of the infringer's invention is no defense.

You can also be sued yourself, even if you are an "innocent" patent infringer. Again, as with trademarks, the lack of an intent requirement is important to the patent infringement discussion. Those accused of patent infringement often react to the accusation by protesting that they couldn't possibly be infringing anything because they have not copied anything. They protest that they are using their own original equipment and that they had no knowledge of the other person's patent, and so they ask how they can infringe what they did not copy. In so doing, they make the mistake of assuming that liability for patent infringement requires them to have acted with some kind of intent – to have purposefully attempted to duplicate someone else's invention with knowledge that they were doing it. They assume that originality

of genesis is a defense. It is not. If you are making, using, or selling a patented invention, the patent holder can sue you for patent infringement and potentially win, even if you've never heard of them or their patent before, and even if you invented your invention without copying theirs. This underscores the importance of performing a freedom-to-operate search prior to committing valuable resources to a new invention.

A patent obtained in the U.S. is only effective in the U.S., and thus a company with a U.S. patent can only sue infringers in the U.S. and its territories.

To sue infringers in other countries, a company would have to obtain patents in those countries. There is no single-source available from which to obtain global patent or trademark protection; you must file in each country. Certain filings, such as those under the Patent Cooperation Treaty, may be made to begin the patent process in a number of countries simultaneously. But ultimately each country where protection is sought must get its due.

Note that patent infringement lawsuits can be brought against anyone who makes, sells, or merely *uses* an infringing product. This means that if you make a product that infringes my patent and sell it to your customers, I can sue you for making and selling the infringing product, and I can sue your customers for using it. In fact, as you might imagine owing to the obvious hardship it would inflict on customer relations, the threat that a patent holder might bring suit against an infringer's customers can serve as an important motivator during the course of settlement discussions in a suit against the seller.

Considerations & Trends

Patents are part of a company's total intellectual property strategy. Any company that is advancing the state of the art in any area should be filing patents for all of its inventions and advancements. Companies that are inventing should have a well regulated, strategically integrated patent policy. Why? Because your competition is patenting.

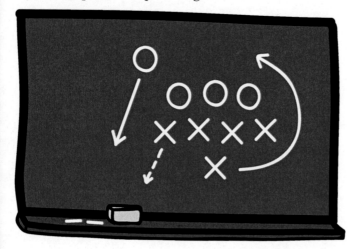

The USPTO issues three to four thousand patents each week. That's a million new U.S. patents every 5 or 6 years.

To put these numbers in perspective, consider that U.S. patent number 1,000,000 was issued in 1911, and number 2,000,000 was issued 24-years later, in 1935. So, a century ago, during the height of the industrial revolution, it took 24-years to issue a million patents. Needless to say, the pace has increased. U.S. patent number 6,000,000 was granted in 1997 and number 7,000,000 was granted just over eight years later in 2006. Patent number 8,000,000 issued in August 2011. We've gone from a million patents every generation, to a million patents every 5 or 6 years.

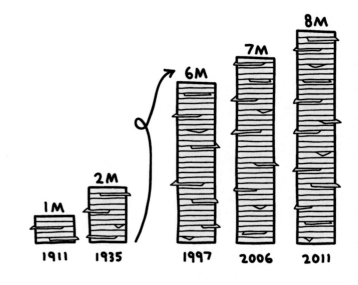

Final Thoughts on Patents

You are strongly advised to give careful consideration to the patent landscape in your field as an essential step in the formulation of product roadmaps and strategies. Even if you don't think you will want or need to obtain any patents yourself, consider the risk of deploying a new product or service without reviewing the likelihood that it infringes the issued or pending patents of your competitors.

COPYRIGHTS

What You Will Learn...

Turn on your computer and surf the internet for a while. Nearly everything displayed to you during that process is copyrighted. Turn on your TV or read a magazine. Non-stop copyrights as far as the eye can see. Copyright is by far the most throughly deployed form of IP in existence. This chapter discusses what a copyright is, how to obtain copyright protection, and what happens when copyright is infringed.

Copyrights protect works of authorship that are fixed in a tangible medium of expression. The subject matter of copyright includes literature, poetry, software, music, lyrics, scripts, screenplays, choreography, photography, motion pictures, graphics, sculptures, paintings, audiovisual works, sound recordings, architectural works, and just about all other similar things. If you author lots of creative content, you should be thinking about copyrights.

Obtaining Copyright Protection

In the U.S., copyright protection applies automatically when you create a work of authorship. No formalities are required to obtain copyright protection. Copyright protection starts from the moment you write something down or hit they keys on your keyboard or put paint to canvas.

No copyright notice is required. You are welcome to put a copyright notice – "© 2013 Purple Monkey Volcano, Inc." perhaps – on anything that is copyrightable as soon as you have created it, but that has no effect on the copyrightability of the work. The presence of a copyright notice on a work of authorship may scare some would-be copyists away, but its presence or absence has virtually no effect on your ability to sue those who do copy.

Federal Copyright Registration
Preferred

Copyright protects works of authorship from the moment of their creation. When you create a work of authorship, an unregistered copyright automatically applies to that work. But the problem with unregistered copyrights is that you cannot sue anyone for infringing them. Federal copyright registration is not necessary to establish a copyright, but registration is necessary to *enforce* a copyright against an infringer in court.

In the U.S., copyright infringement lawsuits may only be brought in federal court – unlike with trademarks, there is no state law copyright action. Without a federal registration, therefore, a company cannot bring a lawsuit for infringement of its copyrights. It is strongly advisable for you to obtain federal copyright registrations for the works of authorship you care about.

This will ensure that you can actively police the copying of your content by others and act quickly to stop it. Moreover, registering copyright within 90 days after the publication of the underlying work of authorship confers numerous advantages on the copyright holder, such as the ability to seek additional damages and enjoy additional presumptions at trial.

To obtain a copyright registration, you submit an application to the copyright office at the U.S. Library of Congress along with two copies of the work of authorship.

While technically the copyright registration application is a bona fide application that can in some circumstances be rejected, the copyright registration process is not at all similar to the patent and trademark processes discussed above in that the copyright application process is not terribly adversarial. The vast majority of properly formed copyright registration applications are accepted without comment from the copyright office. Only in very rare circumstances will the registrar reject a copyright application on substantive grounds.

Recall that registering a copyright requires submission of two copies of the copyrighted work to the copyright office. Upon submission, these copies essentially become a matter of public record as they will be stocked at the library of congress and made available for the public to peruse. This public disclosure means that *any confidential information or trade secrets disclosed in the submitted work will immediately lose trade secret protection!* Prior to submitting works to the copyright office, therefore, take great care to redact or remove any confidential information and trade secrets appearing within.

Unlike many other areas of law, copyright tends to be roughly uniformly structured and applied throughout the modern world. Foreign copyright registration is recommended for those materially engaging in overseas content distribution.

COPYRIGHT INFRINGEMENT

A copyright holder can bring an infringement action against anyone who copies his or her copyrighted work of authorship. An infringing copyist is anyone who actually makes a literal copy of the work, or anyone who creates a substantially similar work after having had access to the original work.

So if, for example, you photocopy or make a digital copy of this book, you have made a literal copy and have thereby committed copyright infringement. Likewise, if you read this book, put it down, and then go away and write a substantially similar book, you have also committed copyright infringement. This doesn't mean you cannot write your own book on intellectual property. It means, however, that now that you have had access to this book, you should not write a book that is so substantially similar to this book that your book is essentially a copy of mine, as that could constitute an infringement.

I do not own the concept of writing a book on IP law. I do not even own the ideas expressed in this book. Ideas and concepts cannot be owned. My copyright extends only to the particular selection and order of topics and words I've used to express the ideas and concepts in this book. Re-write my book in your own words taking care to depart sufficiently from my particular word choice and topical order, and you may not be infringing my copyright in this book.

Exclusive Rights

A copyright holder enjoys numerous exclusive rights, the right of reproduction (copying) being the most widely known. As a copyright holder, you own the exclusive right to reproduce your copyrighted works and you can sue anyone else who makes copies. You also enjoy the right to prevent others from: preparing derivative works (adaptations, for example, and translations) of your work; selling, distributing, leasing, and lending your work; publicly performing your work; and publicly displaying your work.

This means that others may not necessarily copy and re-use your works of authorship that they find on your website, for example, or in your products. Just because copying is easy, doesn't mean it's lawful.

Originality

As discussed above, a person who infringes a patent or a trademark can be liable even if their infringing behavior does not arise from copying. Originality is no defense to patent or trademark infringement claims. That is, you can be liable for trademark or patent infringement even if your accused brand or invention is your own original creation that you've forged all on your own without ever having seen or heard of the trademark or patent you're accused of infringing.

With copyrights, however, the opposite is true. ***Originality is a viable defense to a claim of copyright infringement.*** If you create your work of authorship all on your own without copying another person's copyrighted work (or without violating the access-plus-substantial-similarity rule noted above), then you will probably not be liable for copyright infringement.

Let me be clear: if you were to write a book on your own that *coincidentally* turned out to be a word-for-word clone of this book, you would not be liable for copyright infringement if you could successfully demonstrate that you had never read or had access to this book beforehand. Your original creation would be a good defense against any claim of infringement from me, no matter how statistically unlikely it may be.

Copyright Duration

Copyright protection for works authored by natural persons (human beings) lasts until December 31 of the year in which the 70th anniversary of the author's death occurs – in shorthand: life of the author plus 70 years. Copyright protection for works authored by non-natural persons (companies), also called "works for hire," lasts for the earlier of 95 years from publication date or 120 years from date of creation for works that are never published.[8]

The astute reader will marvel at the incredibly long duration of protection enjoyed by copyright holders. Recall that patents last for only 20 years from the date the application is filed. And trademarks, while of potentially eternal duration, do actually cease to be enforceable when the underlying brand is no longer used in commerce. Not so with copyrights. Copyrights last for more or less a century regardless of the extent to which the underlying work of authorship is made, used, sold, or enjoyed. Copyrights last long enough that the beneficiaries of their protection almost always include the children, grandchildren, and sometimes great-grandchildren of the author. Perhaps this is a trade-off for the fact that copyright does not protect against innocent infringement, as discussed above.

Interestingly, when I went to law school and first began earnestly learning about copyrights in 1991, the time periods that U.S. law provided for copyright protection for works for hire were not 95, but 75 years from the date of first publication, and not 120, but 95 years from date of creation for unpublished works. What do you suppose happened between then and now to cause these statutory durations to expand?

These durations only apply to works authored after 1976. For older works, computing copyright duration is a matter of considerably greater complexity.

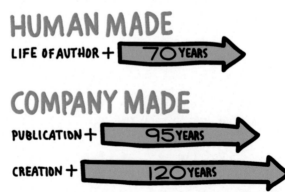

HUMAN MADE
LIFE OF AUTHOR + 70 YEARS

COMPANY MADE
PUBLICATION + 95 YEARS
CREATION + 120 YEARS

Steam Boat Willy

In 2002, *Steam Boat Willy*, the first major film in which the venerable Mickey Mouse character appears, was about to celebrate the 75th anniversary of its release. Under the copyright law in force at that time, which dictated a 75-year duration for copyrights held by companies, the copyright for *Steam Boat Willy* was set to expire on the 75th anniversary of its release. This would have thrust the movie into the public domain for all to copy and enjoy.

The copyright to *Steam Boat Willy* was (and is) of course held by the Walt Disney company. It is probably safe to say that the folks at Disney were troubled by the prospect of *Steam Boat Willy's* entering the public domain. It could be argued that when Steam Boat Willy enters the public domain, the copyright on the Mickey Mouse character could be considerably weakened. Once the movie enters the public domain, it is possible that all imagery from the movie, including still shots of Mickey himself, could be freely copied without threat of infringement claims. In 2002, Mickey Mouse was threatening to join the ranks of Lady MacBeth, Robin Hood, and Count Dracula as characters in the public commons, and would thereby become freely available for anyone to use for any purpose.

The folks at Disney lobbied their local congressperson, who incidentally was (the now late) Sonny Bono of *Sonny and Cher* fame, to prevail upon him to attempt to prevent Mickey Mouse, an American national treasure, from entering the public domain. Congressman Bono thereupon presented legislation to the U.S. congress to lengthen by 20 years the statutory duration of copyright protection for works like Steam Boat Willy. And that legislation, now known as the Sonny Bono Copyright Extension Act of 2002, easily passed, extending the duration of copyright on works for hire from 75 years to 95 years.

Amid accusations that the U.S. had dipped from capitalist democracy into oligarchic plutocracy, Disney, a wealthy and powerful organization, commiserated with one of its own brethren, Rep. Bono, to cause the rules that govern us all to be changed to its considerable financial favor. Mickey Mouse was saved from the hands of the public for another 20 years. We shall see what happens when Mickey's first film reaches its 95th anniversary in 2022.

One thing is certain: While there are those who dislike IP, few of them work in Hollywood or Washington D.C.

UNCOPYRIGHTABLE SUBJECT MATTER

Some things cannot be copyrighted. Let's examine a few.

Ideas, facts, and titles are not subject to copyright protection. For example, stock quotes, sports scores, raw data, historical facts, and recipe ingredients are generally not copyrightable in and of themselves. Functional systems and methods are not copyrightable, but they may be patentable as inventions.

Ideas

Ideas are not copyrightable subject matter. No copyright protection subsists in pure ideas; copyright only protects specific expressions of ideas with particular words and pictures. This book is protected by copyright in that it would be an infringement to copy my particular selection of words and topics. But the idea of IP, or the idea of a book about IP, is not protected.

Facts

$$2+2=4$$

Facts are also not copyrightable. To obtain copyrightability, a work of authorship must evince some minimal level of authored creativity. Raw facts, by their very nature, are devoid of creativity and are therefore not protected by copyright. Copyright only attaches to raw facts and data under two circumstances: (i) when described in a creative way; and (ii) when compiled, arranged, or selected in a creative way.

It is a **fact** that as I write this sentence I am sitting on a plane from Tampa to San Francisco. If this plane were to crash and I were to survive and write a book about the experience, I would most assuredly own a copyright in that book and its creative expression of the germinal facts of the crash. But I would not own a copyright in the facts themselves. You and everyone else would be freely at liberty to extract, reproduce, and write books about those facts right alongside mine.

I might also be able to convince someone to buy "my story." But that would not mean that the facts contained in my story would somehow belong to me or the person who bought my story. I would merely have sold the buyer the right to claim they were telling my authorized recitation of the events of the crash. Regardless of this, you would be free to use the underlying facts in any way you chose. You would not, however, be free to make word-for-word copies of the creative expression of my story in my book or anyone else's book for that matter. You can use the facts, but you must describe them in your own words.

Compilations of facts and raw data can contain elements in the manner of their presentation that meet the minimal creativity standards necessary for copyright protection to attach. Consequently, copyright can protect groupings of facts to the extent that the factual data are selected, coordinated, or arranged by the author in such a way that the resulting work as a whole rises to the level of an original work of authorship. The uncopyrightable facts and data themselves are only protected by copyright when presented in their creatively selected, coordinated, or arranged form.

Works Lacking Any Creativity

No copyright protection applies to works created without the exertion of at least a modicum of creativity.[7] One famous example of an unprotectable work would be the phone book. The phone book is merely an alphabetized list of names and phone numbers. Courts have ruled that the phone book does not rise to the requisite level of creativity to warrant copyright protection. Add a little creativity, however, and you will have crossed the line into copyrightable territory. The white pages are not copyrightable; the yellow pages most certainly are.

Titles

No copyright protection subsists in the title of a single work of authorship. If you were to write a book called, "The Rhyme of the Ancient Purple Monkey Volcano," you would own a copyright in the text of the book, but you would not own a copyright in the book's fancy title. You would be powerless to prevent others from writing another book with the same title. (Incidentally, the title of a single work is also not protectable as a trademark.) But if you were to create and brand a series of books, a serialized collection of stories, a magazine or periodical, a television *series*, a string of movies, or additional merchandise such as action figures, for example, then the name of these things could become protectable under trademark, and possibly copyright, theories.

For example, when the original *Star Wars* movie was first released, its title, "Star Wars," was probably not protectable and, at the time, you or I could probably have published our own book or movie titled *Star Wars* without too much fear of reprisal. (We could not have gotten away with closely copying the story or the characters from the movie, mind you, but the title would probably have been fair game.) Since then, however, the "Star Wars" title has risen to the level of a famous brand name

7

This particular concept of creativity is often confusingly referred to by some authorities as "originality," a term I prefer to use in reference to genesis.

and, due to its widespread use on a series of works of authorship, toys, games, and numerous other products, it is now undoubtedly a protectable trademark and may also in some sense be protectable by copyright. Suffice it to say that, today, any attempt to use "Star Wars" as the title of a book or movie would undoubtedly be met with a measure of legitimate opposition.

The Fair Use Doctrine

Your employees may come to you some day and say, "We copied this thing from someone else and we put it in our product and we shipped it. But that's ok, because it's a fair use." How do you respond? It is true that sometimes a copy is not a copyright infringement because it is a fair use. But when is that?

The inimitable Dr. Seuss hath written, "And so when you step, step with care and great tact. And remember that life's a great balancing act." The great symbol for the law is the scales of justice, because answering any sufficiently interesting question is difficult and requires the *weighing and balancing* of numerous facts, veins of evidence, and lines of reasoning. Rarely is this concept of balancing more applicable than in the assessment of whether or not an act of copying constitutes a fair use under copyright law.

"Fair use" describes a copy that might constitute copyright infringement under most circumstances, but is instead deemed to be non-infringing under certain exceptional circumstances. The Copyright Act does not clearly define a fair use; it merely lists the factors to be considered by a court in determining whether a use made of a copyrighted work in a particular case is a fair one. The lack of a bright line test for determining whether a copy qualifies as a fair use can complicate the predictability of a particular case's resolution.

You probably do not require intimate familiarity with the details of the machinery a court would employ to determine a fair use. But let's walk through an overview of the process, so when your copyist employees do present this issue to you, you can ask them the right questions.

Fair Use: Four Factors

The Copyright Act provides four factors that courts must weigh and consider on a case by case basis in determining whether a copy is a fair use. The four fair use factors to be considered are:

1 The purpose and character of the use, which has 3 sub-tests:

- Whether the copy is of a commercial or nonprofit nature;

- Whether the copy is for criticism, comment, parody, news reporting, or noncommercial teaching, scholarship, or research; and

- Whether the copy is transformative of the original work.

2 The nature of the copyrighted work;

3 The amount of the copyrighted work that has been copied in relation to the copyrighted work as a whole; and

4 The effect of the copy upon the potential market for the copyrighted work.

These four statutory factors may not be treated in isolation. All must be explored, and the results weighed together. Unfortunately, fair use jurisprudence reflects considerable imprecision in how courts apply the factors.

Fair Use Factor One: Purpose & Character of the Use

Under the first factor of the fair use test, noncommercial use of an infringing work weighs in favor of a finding of fair use, whereas a commercial use weighs against fair use. Every commercial use of copyrighted material is presumptively not a fair use. Note that if you distribute copyrighted material as a part of a for-profit enterprise, it is regarded as a commercial use even if no actual profit is earned.

Also under the first factor, a copy will be more likely to be found to be a fair use if it has been made for the purposes of commercial or noncommercial criticism, comment, parody, news reporting, or noncommercial teaching, scholarship, or research. You are generally entitled to make copies of things in order to criticize, make fun of, or study them.

A fair use is almost never found when copying is for the purpose of saving users the expense of purchasing additional authorized copies.

The fair use inquiry sometimes focuses on whether the new work merely supersedes and replaces the original creation, or whether and to what extent it is "transformative," altering the original with new expression, meaning, or message. The more transformative the new work, the less will be the significance of other factors, like commercialism, that may weigh against a finding of fair use. A sufficiently transformative use, even if it is commercial in nature, can be a fair use. One indication of a transformative use would be that the copy is not a substitute for the original work in the marketplace. Another is that the copy somehow becomes a driver of interest in the original work. Sometimes, this can be accomplished with careful attention to full and proper citation of the source of the copied work. Citation alone cannot forestall a finding of infringement, but fair use under this first factor can be demonstrated by showing that the proper credits were given to the author of the original work and that the portions reproduced were for a limited purpose not in direct competition with the owner of the copyrighted work.

Plagiarism

Please observe that citation is not a fair use factor. That is, dropping a footnote to indicate the source of the copied material does not necessarily transform an infringing copy into a fair use. It may relieve you from being labelled a plagiarist, but it does not undo copyright infringement. I have had numerous clients over the years, however, who were more inclined to pursue copyright infringement claims against copyists who omitted the citation. "If they had only given me credit for the work they copied, I wouldn't sue them," goes the typical attitude. So copyists take heed: sometimes a "thank you" is enough.

Fair Use Factor Two: Nature of the Original Work

In general, the more creative elements of a work of authorship are entitled to greater protection against copying than the less creative elements. A work that is authored for the purpose of benefiting from the exploitation of copyright is entitled to greater protection than material that would be created regardless of profit from the exploitation of copyright. In addition, copies of informational works are more likely to be deemed to be a fair use than copies of purely fictitious works. Copyright protection is narrower, and the corresponding application of the fair use defense greater, in the case of factual works than in the case of works of fiction or fantasy. If a work is more appropriately characterized as entertainment, it is less likely that a defense of fair use will be accepted.

Fair Use Factor Three: Amount & Substantiality of Portion Copied

There are few absolute rules as to how much or how little of a copyrighted work may be copied in order to maintain a finding of fair use. This factor has both quantitative and qualitative components. It has been held that a use is unfair where the quoted materials form a substantial percentage of the copyrighted work or where the quoted material is "essentially the heart of" the copyrighted work. In any case, copying all or most of the entire copyrighted work often precludes a finding of fair use.

A small degree of copying is sufficient to transgress fair use if the copying is the essential part or, as mentioned, the "heart" of the copyrighted work. The U.S. Supreme Court has held that copying a mere two paragraphs from an entire book for the ostensible purpose of comment and criticism was **not** a fair use where the book was Gerald Ford's memoirs and the two copied paragraphs were those discussing Ford's reasoning for the Nixon pardon. The Court more or less suggested that the disclosures in these two paragraphs were the only reason people would be interested in purchasing Ford's memoirs, and, therefore, that publishing them in a book review would obviate the need to purchase the book.

Fair Use Factor Four: Effect of the Use on the Potential Market

A finding of fair use can be denied when copying would result in an adverse impact on the potential market for the original work. The mere absence of measurable pecuniary damage does not require a finding of fair use, however. The *potential* for economic harm to the copyright holder is enough.

Fair Use Summary

Don't let anyone tell you that they can predict whether a particular copy will be likely to be regarded as a fair use or not. After reading the above summary of the fair use rules, could you predict the outcome of any particular set of facts? Beware those who engage in copying under the fair use banner without benefit of a thorough legal analysis.

TRADE SECRETS

What You Will Learn...

Got a secret? Want to protect it? This chapter covers what trade secrets are, how to obtain them, and how they are misappropriated.

Of the various forms of available IP protection, trade secrets tend to be the easiest to grasp. That's because since childhood most of us have learned two important things about secrets: 1. how to keep them, and 2. how not to keep them. Luckily, it doesn't take much more than that to get the hang of dealing with trade secrets in a business context.

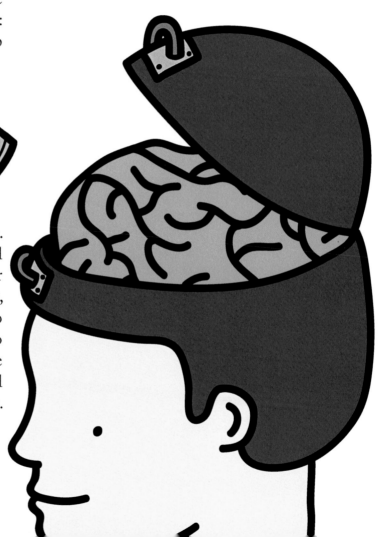

A trade secret is a piece of proprietary information that derives its commercial value because it has been kept secret from competitors. Unlike the other forms of IP, no governmental body registers trade secrets or verifies their status or standing. To create a trade secret, you just have to keep it secret and you have to make sure you disclose it only to others who are obligated to keep it secret. If you do these things successfully, and someone tries to steal your secret, you can probably make them stop.

Nomenclature

The law recognizes subtle differences between so-called "proprietary information," "confidential information," and trade secrets. While you may see these terms used interchangeably in certain contexts, trade secrets are in fact a subset of confidential information, which is in turn a subset of proprietary information.

Proprietary information refers to all of the information that you own, whether you consider it to be secret or not. **Confidential information** is proprietary information that provides competitive value to you because it is secret – not generally known or readily ascertainable by others in your industry – and because you have made reasonable efforts to keep it secret. Finally, **trade secrets** are particular items of confidential information that are more sensitive and more valuable

than run-of-the-mill confidential information. Trade secrets typically include manufacturing techniques, engineering know-how, formulae, recipes, algorithms, methods, software logic, and similar items that are core components of a company's competitive advantage. The primary factor distinguishing confidential information from trade secrets is the duration of their value: trade secrets tend to be core assets that are employed in a business continuously over a long period of time, whereas confidential information tends to be more fleeting in its usefulness and is likely to become outdated more quickly. Trade secrets typically become *more valuable* with age; other confidential information typically becomes *less valuable* with age.

A soft drink company's special recipe for its product would probably constitute a trade secret, as would the specialized knowledge of bottling techniques practiced by its engineers. The same company's confidential information – not rising to the level of trade secrets – would include the wholesale prices at which it purchases supplies, for example, and the identities of the candidates it is considering for its open CEO spot. As another example, a company's trade secrets might include its special software algorithm for establishing the most profitable retail prices for its goods and services. The same company's non-trade secret confidential information, however, would include the particular retail prices it has established for next quarter, for example. While the software algorithm contributes to the long term value of the company's competitive advantage, the quarterly schedule of prices is more fleeting and its secrecy is less critical to the company's long-term success.

The importance of differentiating confidential information from trade secrets becomes clear when your key employees depart to go work for your competition. In jurisdictions where noncompete agreements are upheld, knowledge of confidential information alone may not support enforcement of a noncompete agreement against a departing employee, whereas knowledge of trade secrets might support such enforcement.

The remainder of this chapter uses the term trade secret for convenience. The discussion is, for the most part, equally applicable to confidential information.

OBTAINING TRADE SECRET PROTECTION

If you want trade secrets, you must create trade secrets. How do you do that? By keeping your secrets secret. That's it.

It turns out, one of the best ways to ensure no one copies your idea is not to tell them. [8] If you work reasonably hard at protecting the secrecy of information that has value to you because no one else knows it or can easily get it, then you have probably created a bona fide trade secret that will be protected from misappropriation.

In order to be given protection under trade secret law, information must be the subject of efforts to protect its secrecy. Information that is not subject to affirmative efforts to protect secrecy can lose trade secret protection. Just claiming that information is a trade secret is not enough; marking confidential documents with a "confidential" stamp is nice, for example, but comprises only one step in what should be a more comprehensive process for protecting secrecy. Such a process might also include maintaining only a limited number of copies of sensitive documents, storing trade secrets in restricted areas, tightly controlling access to confidential information with sign-out sheets and electronic passwords as well as encryption, disclosing secret information only to people in your company who need to know it in order to carry out their work, establishing policies that prevent employees from inadvertently disclosing trade secrets in published papers or at conferences, and, perhaps most importantly, executing nondisclosure agreements with anyone who is not already under an obligation to protect the secrecy of shared information.

Nondisclosure Agreements

Nondisclosure agreements (NDAs) must be executed with everyone outside your company with whom you intend to share trade secrets. Failing to do so can result in the loss of trade secret protection for all information shared. The reasoning for this is simple. Trade secret law protects secrets! Information shared with anyone not legally obligated to keep your secrets is by definition no longer a secret. So make it a habit to get NDAs in place with every third party with whom you share trade secrets. [9]

Be sure the provisions of your NDA do not inadvertently deprive you of the full duration of trade secret protection available. Many NDAs, as with most contracts, recite limited periods of time during which they are in full force and effect. Unfortunately, such a limited period may not always coincide with the length of time the underlying information could otherwise have enjoyed the benefit of trade secret protection. In short, the period of time during which the recipient of trade secret information under an NDA

[8] You can go too far here, however, and let paranoia get the best of you. Secrecy of special technical know-how can of course engender years of success. But secrecy of a new idea for a business can only properly go so far. If you're going to launch a new business, at some point you're going to have to tell someone about it! See the next footnote.

[9] Not every meeting needs to involve the disclosure of trade secrets. Most potential investors and business partners are unlikely to sign an NDA at the very first meeting they take with you, until you've piqued their interest. Consider preparing two presentations of your business opportunity: a public version and a secret version. Reserve your insistence on an NDA only for the latter.

should be obligated to maintain the confidentiality thereof should be unlimited; the nondisclosure and nonuse provisions of the NDA should survive any termination of the rest of the agreement until such time as the underlying information no longer qualifies for trade secret protection. Again, the reasoning for this is simple: if you contractually obligate me to keep your secrets for only two years, then when that two-year period ends I will be at liberty to divulge your secrets to others and your secrets will be, by definition, no longer protected as secrets.

x _Brent_

THIS IS OUR LITTLE SECRET

Duration of Trade Secret Protection

Trade secret protection lasts for as long as you maintain the secrecy of the underlying information. Trade secret protection can therefore outlast all other forms of IP protection. Coca Cola had maintained the recipe for its flagship soft drink a closely guarded trade secret since the mid-1800's.

As noted above, however, secrecy must be diligently maintained. Only a single unprotected disclosure can destroy trade secret protection forever. While you may question how an inadvertent disclosure could ever matter, consider that if you later sue someone for misappropriating the trade secret, the defendant will make it a mission to unearth evidence demonstrating even a single prior breach of secrecy.

Misappropriation of Trade Secrets

You can bring an action for trade secret misappropriation against anyone who misappropriates your trade secret – anyone who takes it without permission. To be liable for misappropriation, the defendant must have **taken** your secret from you. If they come up with it on their own, you're out of luck. Original genesis is by definition not a misappropriation. Even though you're keeping something secret, others are entitled independently to discover the same thing, as long as they do so entirely on their own without taking the information from you. In this way, trade secrets resemble copyrights more than trademarks and patents; a defendant's assertion that she developed the information independently of any reference to your trade secrets can prevent a finding of misappropriation.

Final Thoughts Trade Secrets

Admit it: you're keeping secrets. You're keeping secrets that give you an advantage in the marketplace. C'mon, you know it's true. It might be the contents of your salesforce.com database; it might be your recipe for the next thing since sliced bread.

Oh yeah, you've got secrets alright. The question is: are you going to protect them? It'd be a shame if anything were to happen to them. But look, we both know you've got secrets and we both know what you can do to protect them. Understand and employ the teachings of trade secret law. There, that didn't hurt. Did it?

CREATION & OWNERSHIP

What You Will Learn...

When you engage in the creative, innovative, artistic, or inventive process, how do you know what sort of IP assets you've created and which IP rights might attach to them? Moreover, who owns the IP you create? This chapter helps you understand how to identify IP rights and determine who owns them.

IDENTIFYING THE IP YOU'VE CREATED

Let's suppose you were to sit down right now and draft a design and functional specification document for a new product, say, an electric car. What forms of IP would spring into existence or otherwise be available to protect this new creation?

Trademarks

If you elect to think up a brand name for your new car, you can file a trademark application on the brand. The application would be styled an intent-to-use application until you submit a specimen showing the new mark in use as the brand name of the car. Moreover, if you perceive the overall exterior or interior design of your car as rising to the level of having the power to identify you or your company as the unique source of electric cars in the marketplace, then your design might qualify for trade dress protection and you can file a trademark application on that as well.

Patents

Patent protection could be available for any useful, novel, and nonobvious inventions disclosed in your document. You can file the entire document as a provisional patent from which one or more nonprovisional patent applications could later be converted, or you can file individual nonprovisional applications for each invention as an initial move, skipping the provisional patents altogether. One of your nonprovisional patent applications could be a design patent application, protection under which might be available respecting any novel and nonobvious designs reflected in your document. Each patentable invention or design in the document will lose patent protection in the U.S. if you do not file a patent application within one year after first disclosing the invention publicly, selling it, or offering it for sale.

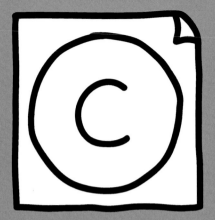

Copyrights

Your document would be copyrighted automatically from the moment of its creation (regardless whether it is fixed on paper or merely typed or drawn on a computer). You can register the copyright by sending in an appropriate application to the copyright office, taking care to redact or remove any secret material from the submitted copies of the work. Alongside your copyright on the document as a whole, it is possible that subsets or portions of your document could be recognized as separate works of authorship subject to individual copyright protection -- and could thus become the subject of separate copyright applications -- such as the nonfunctional or ornamental features of the design of the car.

Trade Secrets

As an initial matter, you can easily elect to keep your document and its contents a secret by, well, just keeping it a secret, which means not disclosing it to the public and only showing it to those who owe you a duty of confidentiality, such as your executive employees and other people who have signed an NDA. Be aware, however, that once you eventually manufacture and sell the car reflected in the design document, any features that are observable to anyone looking at the car will thereupon lose any secrecy protections.

Availability of Multiple Forms of IP Which Should You Choose?

As you may have noticed, the four areas of IP law that we have discussed – trademarks, patents, copyrights, and trade secrets – share a certain amount of overlap as to their subject matter. Any software systems in your electric car, for example, can conceivably be protectable by three kinds of IP: patents, copyrights, and trade secrets. Indeed, many trade secrets, because they are often written down as documents or computer files, are potentially also protectable as either copyrightable works or patentable inventions. Product designs can also conceivably be protected by trade dress, design patents, and copyrights. Herein lies an opportunity for many businesses to engage in a bit of strategy. You may elect to protect certain items with different forms of IP depending on the particular facts and circumstances of your business and your competitive landscape.

If duration of protection is important, consider that patents last for 20 years and copyrights last for 90 years (in many cases), while trademarks and trade secrets potentially last forever. If scope of protection is important, consider that copyright and trade secret law both permit suits against only intentional copyists and thieves, while patent and trademark law both permit suits against even innocent infringers.

Another trade-off between secrecy and patents is of course that patents are disclosed to the public and patented inventions automatically become part of the public domain when the patent expires, whereas trade secrets can be maintained in perpetuity.

In terms of the difficulty with which IP rights can be obtained, patents -- design patents or utility patents -- are much more difficult to obtain than other forms of IP protection; to warrant patent protection the invention must be novel and nonobvious, after all. Trademark protection is probably the next hardest to obtain, followed by copyright. As should be obvious by now, trade secrets are easiest.

OWNERSHIP

So you've drafted your design document for your electric car, and, as illustrated above, it is veritably brimming with all manner of intellectual property. Who owns the IP you've just created? The answer depends on your employment status.

Ownership by Creator

If you create IP on your own completely outside the context of any employment relationships, you as an individual person most likely enjoy unfettered ownership of the IP you've created including the right to apply for any statutory protection in your own name.[10] As its owner, you would be free to deal in your IP by assigning it or licensing it to others and to sue infringers.

Ownership by Employers vs. Employees

While the rules of ownership can vary across the forms of IP, in general the employer automatically owns trade secret information, copyrightable works of authorship, patentable inventions, and trademarkable brands created by full-time, W2 employees working within the scope of their employment at the employer's behest using the employer's time and resources. The employee in this situation owns nothing, not even necessarily the right to claim credit for having created the IP. [11] Works of authorship created by *bona fide* employees are called "works for hire."

Ownership becomes harder to predict with certainty respecting IP created by part-time employees, employees who create work-related IP on their own time and equipment, or those who use their employer's resources to create IP that is noncompetitive or unrelated to the employer's business (such as, for example, using the computer your employer provides to you at work to write a novel that has nothing to do with your job). Each case in this realm will turn on its specific facts -- making predictability all but impossible -- unless the ownership rules are decided ahead of time by employers and employees. Well-written employment agreements can forestall uncertainty by delineating bright-line rules governing IP ownership for these various situations.

> **10** Only people and companies can own IP. Paintings prepared by animals, for example, are owned by whomever owns the animal. Likewise, IP "created" by computers or other machines, no matter how autonomously, will be owned by the owner of the machine.

> **11** Notwithstanding this fact, only natural humans, not companies, can be named as inventors on patents, so even when the invention and patent are owned by a company, the human inventor(s) will still be identified as the inventors. Not so with any other form of IP.

Ownership by Independent Contractors

In general, non-employee independent contractors own the IP they create except to the extent ownership is dictated in written agreements between the buyer and the seller. In copyright cases, this is true regardless of any other aspect of the relationship. To be clear: **if anyone who is not your employee creates for you a copyrightable work of authorship, you will not own it unless the independent contractor has executed an assignment agreement**. An example: Suppose you ask me to build you a kitchen table, but we don't sign any written agreement; we just shake hands. I'm not your employee so technically I'm an independent contractor. I build the table and deliver it to you, and you pay me handsomely for it. At the end of the deal, you will own the table and I will keep the money, and, because the table is unlikely to be a copyrightable work of authorship, the law will support that conclusion quite strongly. It's your table; you bought and paid for it.

Now, suppose you ask me to write a book or create a work of art, again only on a handshake with the stated intention that you will own the resulting work of authorship. I create the work product, deliver it to you, and receive payment. Now who owns what?

Surprisingly, I still own the work product, even though you bought and paid for it. And I can keep your money. Because we did not have a written agreement, what you bought and paid for turns out to be only an implied license to use and enjoy the work product I delivered to you in whatever limited manner the circumstances might imply. I still maintain ownership of the underlying work of authorship and I can continue to use it, adapt it, and even sell it to your competitors, multiple times.

Only a written assignment agreement can transfer ownership of copyrightable works from sellers to buyers. Without a written assignment agreement, ownership does not pass and buyers are left with limited rights.

Non-Employee Works for Hire

As noted above, copyrightable works created by full-time employees working within the scope of their employment generally become categorized as works for hire, which means the employer becomes the owner of the work upon its creation and the employee owns nothing. In certain circumstances, works of authorship created by non-employee independent contractors can be designated as works for hire as well. For several reasons, work-for-hire status confers ownership rights on the buyer that are somewhat stronger than that which can be transferred in an assignment agreement.[12] Thus, if available, work-for-hire status is preferable to an assigned copyright.

First, to establish a work for hire from a non-employee independent contractor seller, the buyer must obtain a written agreement signed by the seller in advance of the creation of the work that designates the work as a "specially commissioned work for hire."[13] Second, in order to qualify for work-for-hire status in an independent contractor scenario, the work must be one of the following 9 items: a contribution to a collective work, a part of a motion picture or other audiovisual work, a translation, a supplementary work, a compilation, an instructional text, a test, answers to a test, or an atlas. Given these 9 limited and somewhat obscure categories, it is clear that not everything created by independent contractors can qualify as works for hire.

Historically, IP lawyers have taken a belt and suspenders approach to agreements governing creation and delivery of copyrightable works by including language to the effect that the deliverables would be specially commissioned works made for hire unless the law did not permit such a result, in which case ownership of the deliverables would be assigned to the buyer. Except in California, where only very careful use of work-for-hire language is advised, the belt and suspenders approach remains the norm.

12 For example, copyright assignments are automatically and inalienably revocable after 35 years, whereas works for hire belong to the buyer in perpetuity.

13 These exact words are required.

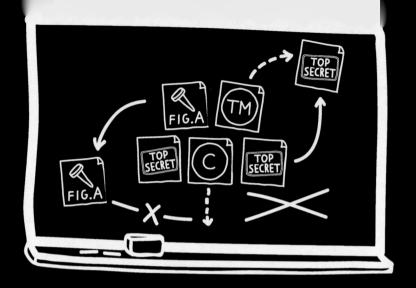

MANAGEMENT & STRATEGY

What You Will Learn...

This chapter discusses how to ensure that the IP you and your employees create can be identified, catalogued, and used.

Every innovative company should establish internal processes and controls for managing IP. Once you have learned the ins and outs of patents, copyrights, trade secrets, and trademarks, you may decide that it is in your best interests to pursue IP protection for your protectable assets. What happens next? How do you go about deciding which assets to protect? How do you determine whether your company has any IP assets worth protecting in the first place? And once you obtain IP protection, how do you keep track of it all? The answers to these questions are nonobvious. You would be surprised at how few companies manage their IP effectively.

IP management is analogous to financial management. Your company (and perhaps your household) probably already realizes considerable benefits from internal practices and controls for monitoring cash flow, tracking spending, and formulating financial strategy. Using a similar system for tracking information and making decisions about IP can be similarly beneficial.

Interestingly, a primary reason why companies (and individuals) pay so much attention to financial matters is that it is mandated by law; everyone and every company making money needs to file an accurate annual tax return at the very least, and some larger companies are required to maintain and report accurate financial records under various securities laws. Not so with IP. There is no Internal Revenue Service or Securities and Exchange Commission to regulate what you do with your IP portfolio or how you manage it. For the most part, you needn't report in detail on the status of your IP to your shareholders or the public. The USPTO and the U.S. Copyright Office will gladly issue IP rights to you on your IP assets. But other than demanding some routine renewal filings, no one at the USPTO will ever be concerned with how or whether you manage or maintain those rights or use them in your business or your life.

Because there is no IRS or SEC to force compliance, responsibility for caring about IP management falls squarely on your shoulders. Consider working through the following steps to ensure your IP is generating maximum value and minimal risk.

IP Disclosure

If you're running a company, IP disclosure is a critical initial step in IP management. Establish a process for the disclosure and inventory of new creations and insist that all employees follow it obsessively. Why? Because you can't protect what you can't see! To best ensure that creative assets get protected by IP, you've got to train your employees to disclose their creations to you so that a global inventory is maintained. What a tragedy it would be for value to bleed out of your company because you never pursued IP protection on a pile of fallow assets that you never knew existed.

Disclosure of copyrightable works is relatively straightforward. Any company whose employees are in the habit of producing copyrightable works of authorship other than software – such as magazine articles, music, photographs, blog entries, and such – ought to have a standard process in place by which these employees send copies of each new work up the management chain so a determination can be made as to whether to send copyright registration applications in to the copyright office in the U.S. or any other jurisdictions.

New brands are unlikely to slip through the cracks and remain inadvertently undisclosed. Brands tend to be developed alongside a larger effort to create a new product or service, so they rarely get created without management involvement or awareness. Nevertheless, every new brand, logo, tagline, and trade dress developed in your company should be passed up the chain for inventory and analysis as to whether and in what jurisdictions trademark registration should be pursued.

For inventions and know-how, use a simple invention disclosure form that collects basic information about each new creation. The invention disclosure form should be simple enough that your engineering staff can fill it out quickly with minimal impact on their time, yet comprehensive enough so that you can later decide whether the new creation is strategically or competitively valuable enough to warrant IP protection. You can also decide at this stage whether the new creation should best be protected as a patentable invention or kept confidential as proprietary information (or, for software, protected as a copyrightable work). Great care must be taken to ensure that all invention disclosures remain strictly confidential until the chosen form of IP is pursued.

Impediments to IP Disclosure

Unfortunately, various factors can impede the IP disclosure process. Filling out an invention disclosure form is more than a simple ministerial duty; it is a grand statement of authorship and responsibility. "Hey everyone, look at me. I am advancing the state of the art!" For all but those most at ease with self-promotion, this task can be daunting.

We humans come from schools of fish and herds of animals for whom blending in with the group is a survival strategy and standing out from the crowd can get you eaten. After millennia of honing our pattern-matching instincts to avoid predators, we favor the boring and we viscerally disdain things that are crazy, unexpected, nonstandard, different, or bizarre. Unfortunately, these are the very features that denominate practically all new inventions and innovations.

We can sometimes feel an instinctive reluctance to stand up and claim credit for new inventions because we're not sure how our claims will be met by those around us. We know that our peers (and our superiors) can, justifiably or not, sometimes feel threatened by our individual successes. Perhaps they cannot imagine their place in a world marked by the changes our new innovation represents. Perhaps we sense their instinctive insecurities. Either way, when someone thinks his ox is about to be gored, it is unrealistic to expect him to be a terribly big fan of the invention (or inventor) doing the goring.

The trick is to celebrate and reward innovation at every level. Let it ring through the halls of your company that those who create IP are to be revered. Your creative staff should know to a certainty that each IP disclosure will be judged on its merits (keeping them anonymous can be useful here). Demand faithful attention to preparing invention disclosures as a job requirement for all creative staff. Consider paying a special bounty to every employee who is named as an inventor on an issued patent. Consider significant salary bonuses for particularly prolific IP creators.

In the long term, your IP assets may be the most valuable holdings in your company, but only if you are aware of them. Do whatever it takes to ensure your IP assets are fully disclosed by those who create them.

DOCUMENTING IP

The IP management function begins with actually building the IP portfolio – collecting and organizing all available documentation about the IP. This corpus of information should include indexes, summaries, descriptions, and actual copies of:

- All of the company's IP assets, IP rights, and data about their genesis (creator, date of creation, etc.);

- All contracts that transfer IP into the company;

- All contracts or instruments that transfer any IP out of the company or impair the company's ownership rights in it; and

- All searches, legal opinions, and analyses regarding the IP's availability, validity, or infringement.

Documenting IP Completeness

Once all information has been collected, assess the completeness of the IP portfolio by verifying that each IP asset is protected by at least one IP right. Verifying at least a one-to-one mapping from assets to rights ensures that the true value of the portfolio will be likely to approach its theoretical maximum.

Remember that many kinds of IP are protectable by more than one kind of IP right. Software, as noted above, can conceivably be protected by patents, copyrights, and trade secrets simultaneously. Thus, while a one-to-one mapping from IP assets to IP rights is nice, a one-to-many result is even better.

Documenting IP Ownership

Review the contracts collected in steps 2 and 3 to verify that all IP assets and IP rights are the subject of at least one written contractual provision having the legal effect of transferring ownership of the IP from its creator to the company. IP ownership is complex and the applicable rules can seem counterintuitive.

Depending on the relationship between the creator and the company, **mere physical delivery of and payment for an IP asset may not automatically cause the asset or its corresponding IP rights to be owned exclusively by the buyer**. Regardless of the intentions or even awareness of the company and the creator, the creator may sometimes retain ownership rights by default under the law. Title defects such as this represent significant risks to IP holders.

The IP manager or auditor must be meticulous about tracking the effective dates of IP ownership transfers to ensure that they have their intended or purported effect. One often overlooked example involves the use of work-for-hire agreements versus assignment agreements. A company cannot be designated as the author/owner of applicable copyrightable subject matter unless a work-for-hire agreement is executed by the creator in advance of the creation of the work. Any later executed agreement can, at best, transfer only an assignment of copyright from the creator. An assignment is a complete transfer of ownership very much akin to a work-for-hire, but with one critical difference: work-for-hire lasts forever, but assignments are inalienably revocable by the assignor for a period starting 35 years, and ending 40 years, after the effective date of the assignment. Check work-for-hire agreements carefully, therefore, to ensure they were executed prior to the creation of the works they purport to govern.

Review all of the company's out-licenses, security agreements, and other liens and encumbrances. Obviously, any exclusive or otherwise significant out-grant on the company's primary IP assets or IP rights could substantially impair the company's ability to conduct business. The results of this analysis can inform the company's business practices to ensure IP value is preserved and not squandered.

Documenting IP Status & Standing

A critical IP management function is to maintain all IP filings in good standing and to keep them current on all ministerial requirements such as the payment of all applicable fees. Important due dates and filing deadlines should be calendared and monitored closely. Areas of particular concern here would be, for example, provisional patents approaching the 1-year anniversary of their filing with no corresponding nonprovisional application in the works; an intent-to-use trademark application approaching the end of its final 6–month extension with no actual use pending; a registered trademark approaching its renewal term; and any office action approaching its response deadline.

Documenting IP Strength

A substantive phase of IP portfolio management, perhaps its very *raison d'être*, is by far the most complex and feeds back into the earlier process of determining which IP assets to protect with IP rights. To obtain and retain strategic value, your IP should be routinely assessed for its offensive and defensive strength. Offensive strength refers to the capability of IP rights to be successfully asserted against infringers in a licensing or litigation context. Defensive strength refers to the ability of an IP portfolio to ward off infringement claims from competitors by eliciting in them the fear of a successful countersuit, as well as the extent to which the company's IP assets themselves do not, in fact, infringe any third party IP rights. Determining strength requires significant review and analysis of the IP assets and rights in the portfolio, in comparison to the IP assets and rights held by relevant competitors, a process that can call for a large investment of time and legal fees to generate validity and infringement opinions.

Final Thoughts on
Management & Strategy

Every year, disappointed shareholders file more cases claiming that management has needlessly impaired the value of the company's IP. Every year, the SEC brings more charges claiming that management has made fraudulent public statements about its IP. Most of the defendants in these cases did nothing wrong intentionally; they are guilty of nothing more than cultivating a lackadaisical attitude toward internal IP processes and controls. The harms they face could easily have been avoided by a modicum of attention to the IP management techniques described above.

IP: BOON OR BANE?

What You Will Learn...

In the early 1990's just before the dawn of the world wide web, Intellectual Property was the very definition of an esoteric subject. The average person in the street didn't know a patent from a potato. Since then, IP has become a mainstream topic of discussion, and that discussion is often heated. Why? This chapter explains a few of the differing viewpoints about IP expressed by the various stakeholders and pundits.

96

Popularity of IP

IP rights have become a thriving form of currency among a large and growing number of market participants. An entire subculture of IP-focused investment banks, auction houses, speculators, and traders (so-called "trolls") has arisen to make a market in IP that did not, until recently, exist. Underlying the growth of this market is a shared understanding of the fundamental reality that IP lawsuits are crushingly expensive – legal fees on a patent case often exceed $1 million from start to finish. Those accused of IP infringement very often agree to settle the lawsuit and opt instead to pay royalties to the IP holder as a much cheaper and more predictable alternative to the exorbitant expense and uncertain outcome of IP litigation. When litigation doesn't settle, it can ultimately result in large damage awards and even injunctions prohibiting infringing behavior. The losing defendant in an IP lawsuit can be ordered to take entire product lines off the market, leaving the winning IP holder with an exclusive, and thus dominant, competitive position.

This power attracts IP holders. Its availability means that more applications to secure IP rights are being filed every year as more companies attempt to establish exclusionary beachheads in what they suppose to be the important technologies of the future. It also leads directly to more IP being asserted more aggressively than ever against potential infringers, who, in response, round out their own IP portfolios in order to bolster defensive counterclaims. Thus, practically all market participants of every stripe feel compelled to obtain IP protection for both offensive and defensive purposes. Today, viable participation in commerce requires very careful attention to the management of the IP function.

Unpopularity of IP

Reasonable minds can (and most definitely do) differ on whether our IP laws create value and whether IP should be used as described in this book. While many, many companies rely heavily on existing IP laws to build assets and forestall competition, an increasingly vocal faction insists that some of our IP laws might have lost touch with certain realities of modern technology and business practices. These complicated issues of public policy continue to attract significant, sometimes heated, attention from all corners. A peaceful resolution has thus far evaded those of us working on these problems.

Nonetheless, the rules for creating and enforcing IP rights have been the law of the land for centuries. Whether one agrees with them or not, these laws set before America's entrepreneurs various nontrivial opportunities to create value and reduce risk. Only you, in concert with your trusted advisors, can determine whether to seize these opportunities or let them lie fallow.

Some critics of IP laws argue that IP tends to engender the wealth of the corporate class at the expense of the sole inventor and the average citizen. Some encourage engagement in what is known variously as the open source movement, the free software movement, or the creative commons movement, in which people agree to share things, to work on them together, and to give the results away for free.

If you are of this mindset, great. But be advised that you cannot give away that which you do not own in the first place. Intellectual property laws provide the framework to identify the owner of any given innovation. Indeed, if it were not for the availability of IP rights,

the underlying IP assets would not necessarily have the same or even *any* value, and there would be nothing to give away and nothing to share. In other words, a free culture could not exist in its most precise capacity without the underlying IP legal regime that provides rules for IP ownership. Proponents of the open movements will, it is hoped, remain mindful that IP law is not the enemy of free culture,[14] it is the substrate upon which free culture resides.

Opinions vary as to whether free culture or existing IP laws are good or bad for civilization. The open source movement has made major strides in recent years. It is axiomatic that if a software engineer wants his or her source code to be viewed and critiqued by a large number of smart people in order quickly to find the bugs in the code and thereby improve it most efficiently, sometimes it makes sense to release the code to the community of interested developers and let the evolutionary forces of large numbers do their magic to rid the code of bugs and faults.

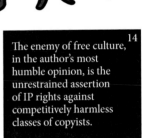

[14] The enemy of free culture, in the author's most humble opinion, is the unrestrained assertion of IP rights against competitively harmless classes of copyists.

Similar strategies can certainly work with art projects and IP assets of all kinds. Many musicians and authors, for example, have realized enormous gains in popularity by literally giving all or part of their works away for free. If balanced properly, free give-aways can actually increase legitimate sales of the same or related products. In the modern digital era, it seems, maximum success or profits can be obtained by promoting a subtle and complicated mixture of brand development, reputation, authenticity, engagement, commentary, and fan base vibrancy, alongside a deliberate and mindful strategy of IP donation versus productization. Ownability as a business concept is perhaps becoming slightly less about the simple accumulation and blatant sale of IP assets and assertion of IP rights, and slightly more about the captivation and cultivation of a tightly coupled relationship between producers and consumers, one that results in bona fide communities built around shared trust and mutual success.

Refining IP Laws

Cries for patent reform grow louder with every passing year. As this book goes to press, moreover, the U.S. Copyright office has suggested that reforms to existing copyright laws may be in order to bring these laws into conformity with modern technological and business trends. The complexity of such undertakings is daunting; legislators endeavoring to redraft decades-old statutes run the risk of creating more problems than they solve. Numerous stakeholders and lobbies on both the creator and consumer sides will voice their opinions and look to have their agendas carried into the foreseeable future. The dynamic can be characterized as a tension between ownership versus access. Those who profit from the creation and sales of IP assets will want tighter IP laws; those who profit from having the ability to access and re-use or re-purpose others' IP assets want a more flexible legal regime.

Please recall from the opening chapter of this book that the Constitutional purpose of our IP laws is to "promote the progress of science and the useful arts." So the question is: How do we best fulfill the Framers' mandate? Which kind of legal regime results in the creation and availability of more IP assets? Which laws incite the greatest inventive, innovative, and artful output? How do we rig the legal system to encourage inventors and artists to create more stuff?

In my personal opinion, the Constitutional mandate would be better served in general if a few changes were implemented. First, patents should be a little bit harder to obtain; patentability should be reserved for only significant advances over the state of the art in a given technology. Minor or incremental improvements should not be awarded patent protection.

Second, the term of copyright protection should be shortened. Patents last for only 20 years, after which the patented invention is injected into the public domain for all to share. Why should copyright last for a century? Wouldn't the public benefit by having access to copyrighted works after a shorter duration?

Finally, the copyright fair use defense should be refined to give primary weight to one of the four fair use factors: the effect that the infringing copy has on the market for the underlying work. If a copyist can show that her copy did not deprive the copyright holder of any sales or profits, shouldn't that forestall a finding of infringement or at least eliminate a monetary damage award?

Only time will tell if statutory revisions like these or others can or should be implemented.

Final Thoughts on IP Reform

I encourage you to remain aware of the availability of opportunities engendered by IP law, and, if you are so inclined, to join the many conversations and communities that have arisen to advance, critique, reform, and replace it. After absorbing the contents of this book, you are encouraged to draw your own conclusions, weigh the various philosophies as against your own personal values, and decide to what extent the IP function matters to you and your company.

If you're going to be an entrepreneur, there will probably be a quiz.

Rock Your Own Ability

It can be lonely and dreadful toting, the life of a creative mind. We, the general public, we don't really get you creative types.

In 1807, an inventor named Robert Fulton went down to the Hudson River in New York City and proclaimed that he intended to build a ship propelled by naught but the power of a steam engine. They laughed at him; they called his project "Fulton's Folly;" and they said it would never work. At the turn of the 19th century, pretty much everyone in the world except Fulton thought that putting an engine on a boat was a bad idea. After all, they cried, we've got paddles and we've got sails! Why on earth do we need a steam engine on our boats? So Fulton's Steamboat, by steaming from NYC up to Albany in less half of the time of a standard sailing vessel, showed conclusively that Fulton was right, and everyone else in the world was wrong. It turned out that engine-powered boats are a pretty good idea. While that may seem ridiculously obvious today, it took a man like Robert Fulton to stand stalwart against the tide of popular opinion to prove it.

Sometimes, even experienced experts lack the foresight to appreciate the power of human creativity. In roughly the year 100 A.D., a Roman engineer named Julius Sextus Frontinus, who had then just successfully completed one of the greatest engineering projects of all time -- the Roman aquaducts, which successfully delivered cold running water from central Italy to the city of Rome -- famously declared, "All that can be invented, has been invented." After all, what more do you need when you've got cold running water?

Inventors, artists, and innovators of all stripes have always confronted the fear, uncertainty, and doubts of those around them. I have little doubt that when the first human left his cave to rub two sticks together in an attempt to make fire, the rest of us -- common grunts and high priests alike -- stood around making fun of him and proclaiming that he was in league with lucifer and imploring him to forget the whole thing and come in to dinner.

Regardless of the pressures you face as an artist or innovator, I hope that this book has guided you through the convoluted terrain of the intellectual property landscape and has made that part of the creative process less daunting than you might previously have thought. Armed with this knowledge, I hope you will go forth with confidence in the ownability of the results of your own ability.

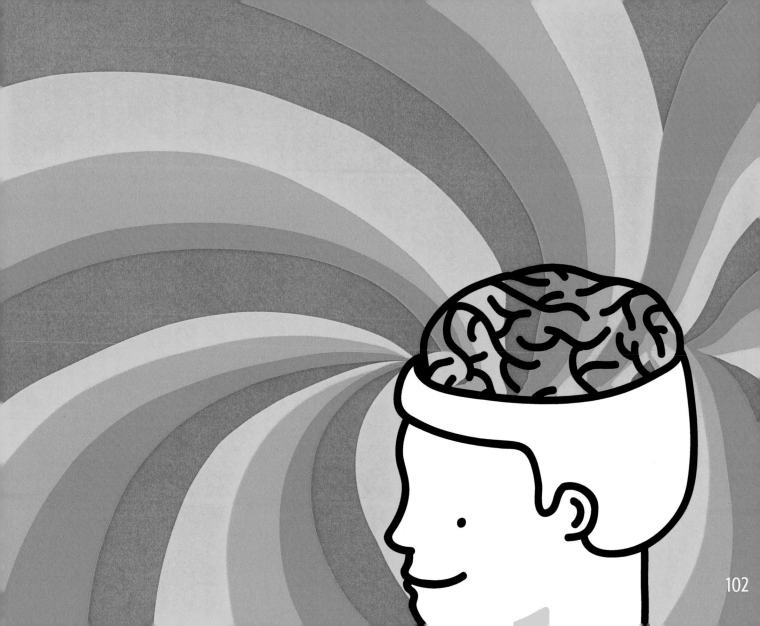

SUMMARY OF IP RIGHTS

	PROTECT	OBTAINED BY	REGISTRATION	DURATION
TM TRADEMARKS	BRANDS, LOGOS	USE IN COMMERCE	OPTIONAL, BUT STRONGLY ADVISED	AS LONG AS USED
FIG.A PATENTS	INVENTIONS	REGISTRATION	MANDATORY	20 YEARS
© COPYRIGHTS	WORKS OF AUTHORSHIP	FIXING THE WORK, TANGIBLY	OPTIONAL, BUT STRONGLY ADVISED	LIFE OF AUTHOR +70 YEARS / 90/120 FOR WORKS FOR HIRE
TOP SECRET TRADE SECRETS	SECRET	KEEPING SECRET	NONE	AS LONG AS KEPT SECRET

EXPECTED LEGAL FEE$

TRADEMARK SEARCH & OPINION LETTER	$1500
US TRADEMARK APPLICATION, PREPARATION & FILING	$1500
PROSECUTION OF TRADEMARK APPLICATION TO REGISTRATION	$1000+
PATENT SEARCH & OPINION LETTER	$2000
PROVISIONAL PATENT DRAFTED BY COUNSEL	$3000-$4000
PROVISIONAL PATENT DRAFTED BY CLIENT & REVIEWED BY COUNSEL	$500-$1000
US NONPROVISIONAL PATENT APPLICATION, PREPARATION, & FILING	$10,000
PROSECUTION OF US PATENT APPLICATION TO ISSUANCE	$1000+
COPYRIGHT REGISTRATION APPLICATION	$500
PREPARATION OF NONDISCLOSURE AGREEMENT	$500
IP PORTFOLIO AUDIT	$500-1000 PER IP ASSET & RIGHT
PATENT VALIDITY & PATENT INFRINGEMENT OPINIONS	$10,000

About The Author

Brent C.J. Britton, Esq. is an entrepreneur, lawyer, scientist, musician.

A Silicon Valley veteran, Britton has been practicing Intellectual Property law since the early 1990's for entrepreneurs, engineers, artists, and companies both large and small.

As the only graduate of the MIT Media Laboratory to become a lawyer, Britton is uniquely skilled in both the art and science of intellectual property. Alongside his master's degree from MIT, Britton holds a Juris Doctor from the Boston University School of Law, and a bachelor's degree in computer science from the University of Maine.

Photo by Robert X. Fogarty, Dear World

A prolific writer and speaker, Britton published his first digital works on the internet in 1984.

Learn more about him at http://en.wikipedia.org/wiki/Brent_Britton.

Made in the USA
San Bernardino, CA
14 February 2015